THE BOOK OF D. BARNES

"AS I WALKED THROUGH THE STREETS OF LOS ANGELES"

Homelessness Was The Springboard to My Destiny

A Memoir

DARRYL BARNES

Copyright © 2013 by Darryl Barnes
Los Angeles, California
All rights reserved
Printed and Bound in the United States of America

Published And Distributed By
Professional Publishing House
1425 W. Manchester Ave., Ste B
Los Angeles, California 90047
323-750-3592
Email: professionalpublishinghouse@yahoo.com
www.Professionalpublishinghouse.com

Cover design: Jay De Vance III
First printing January 2014
978-0-9891960-9-3
Library of Congress Control Number: 2013958248
10987654321

For inquiries, contact the publisher.

Dedication

I dedicate my book to my late mother, Ms. Beverly Williams, and my late god daughter, Amber. May they both rest in peace. I also dedicate this book to the streets of Los Angeles.

I want to acknowledge the people who inspired me to write my book, V. Colbert, E. Rainer, Q. Pettus, and A. Jordan.

To my family and friends, J. Echols, Geneva, Effie and Sandra.

Chapter 1

———◆•✕•◆———

I was living in Atlanta, Georgia. I was in my room watching television. It was about 10:35 p.m. I started getting sleepy and I had to get up at 6:30 a.m. I woke up out of my sleep with my heart beating fast and sweat running from my forehead. I got out of bed, looking around the room; I was in so much fear. After I got myself back to normal, I had to tell myself it was only a bad dream. I went downstairs to get a glass of water. After returning to my room, I looked at the clock. It was 3:45 a.m. I did not intend to go back to sleep. I turned on the television and just lay across my bed.

At 4:45 a.m., I started getting ready for work. As the day went on, I told no one about the nightmare I'd had. I was trying to get it out of my head. After getting off work and making it home, I did what I always did, chilled until about 10:00 p.m. I went to bed and once again at 3:03 a.m. I woke up. I had the same damn dream, same reaction, heart beating like a drum. I jumped out of bed saying, "Why am I having the same dream?" I dropped to my knees and started praying. I turned the television back on and at 5:05 a.m., I got ready for work.

My eyes were bloodshot red as if I'd been up all night drinking. I was so sleepy, but I still went to work. Still, I told no one about my dream. That morning, my mom asked me if I was okay. I told her I was fine. She knew that something was wrong. Mothers that loved and cared for their children knew when something was wrong. I still didn't tell her about the dreams. After getting home, I tried to fight going to sleep. I took a cold shower and made a cup of coffee. It didn't work. By 8:30 p.m., my eyes started to close. The television was still on. By 3:37 a.m., I was awake. I had the same dream. This was driving me crazy. I told myself when I get off work I would tell Mom about this three-day dream.

After getting home, I went downstairs into Mom's room.

"Mom, when you asked me if something was wrong, I didn't want to tell you. I was hoping it would go away, but it didn't; it lasted for three nights. I've been having the same dream. It's like a nightmare. I wake up every night at three something in the morning, with my heart beating fast and sweat running from my forehead. That is why my eyes are so red. I don't go back to sleep. I am scared I might have that dream again."

"What are you dreaming?" she asked.

"It's crazy; all I see is that I'm in Los Angeles, California standing in the middle of the street between two buildings in the dark. Then, I start to walk down the street and I see all of these people trapped in Hell trying to get out, but nobody sees me. This road has no ending. It goes on and on. I wish you could see what I see in this dream, Mom. It's so bad; I am scared to go to sleep at night."

"You need to pray."

"I did. What do you think these three day dreams mean?"

"Maybe it's your destiny. You were walking freely in your dreams and everybody else was trapped."

"What? Go to L. A. California?"

She didn't say anything. After talking to Mom, I went upstairs to my room, thinking about what she said. It never crossed my mind to go to Los Angeles. Before going to sleep, I pulled out the Bible, turned to Revelations and started reading. Then I prayed and went to sleep with the television on. By 5:45 a.m., I woke up to the sound of the alarm clock, and I was so happy I didn't have that dream. Mom asked me if I had the dream, I told her no, kissed her on the cheek and went to work. Today was going to be a good day.

As time moved on, day and night all I saw in my head was Los Angeles, California. It was driving me crazy. I started saving my money and I turned to God for answers. On November 17, 1997, I made up my mind.

"Are you crazy?" Mom asked.

"L.A. is a bad place to go, but Mom, you told me it might be my destiny."

"Yes I did, but I didn't think you would go."

"I have to go. Something is pushing me in that direction. I don't know what it is, Mom. This is the first time in my life I'm going somewhere on a vision. I have to see what's there."

Mom didn't say a word.

That was three weeks ago. I guess she didn't think I was for real. I kissed Mom, and gave her a long hug.

"I love you," she said, as I walked out the door. "Call me when you get there."

"Okay, I love you, too."

Only God knew that this would be the last time that I would see Mom alive.

A friend took me to the bus station. His sentiments were likened to Mom's. "Man, L.A. is like The Wild West. What has you going out there?"

"It's a long story."

After my homeboy dropped me off at the bus station I had time to kill. My bus didn't depart until 6:45 p.m. It was only 5:30 p.m. I started thinking, *What am I going to do? What am I looking for when I get there?* This was the first time I had gone anywhere without a plan. My brain just kept on going and going. Before I knew it, it was 6:45 p.m. They called everyone for the bus to Los Angeles to line up at Gate 8. I stayed in the back of the line.

I wanted to be the last to get on so I could take one last look before I departed.

A few hours later, kids started to run up and down the walkway, playing. One little kid nearby started playing with me.

"C.W., get over here," his mom said. "Leave that man alone."

With fingers in his mouth, C.W. looked at his mom and didn't move. As she started walking toward the back of the bus, he started crying.

I told her it was all right, and I didn't mind playing with him. I love playing with kids. I used to have a job working in a youth center, so it's a part of my life. C.W.'s mom and I started talking. I told her my name. Her name was Pat.

After an hour or two of talking she said, "Wow, it feels like I've known you all of my life. You are a people person."

"Well, I'm just open-hearted." I smiled.

Little C.W. was asleep in his mom's arms.

"Well, it was nice meeting you. I'm going to lay him down and get some sleep myself

"Okay," I said, and went to sleep also.

As days turned to nights, Pat, C.W. and I were like a family. She moved to the back of the bus where I was holding him in my arms. As he slept, I started thinking of my daughter. God knows I've missed her. I tried to be a family man, but it didn't work out. That's another story.

About 1:30 a.m., we reached the border police. Dogs were all over the place. This was my first time seeing this. Everyone had to get off the bus. They were asking everybody if they were an American. After an hour of checking bags, we were allowed back on the bus.

"Damn, that was crazy," I said to myself.

Our next stop was Phoenix, Arizona where I had to say goodbye to Pat and little C.W. She insisted I stay a few days to see if I liked it.

"I would love to, but I have to get to L.A. I wish I could explain it to you, but you wouldn't understand. You would think I was crazy or something. I kissed her and little C.W., and proceeded to get on the bus that was Los Angeles bound. She gave me her info and told me to call and come back this way. I didn't make any promises I just said okay. It was hard for me to turn my back on them, but I had to; I couldn't let anything get in the way of my mission.

It was about 8:30 p.m. on a Friday night when I heard people talking on the bus. I was asleep, but my ears were open. As I opened my eyes and looked out of the window, there was Downtown Los Angeles. "Oh my, God, I'm here," I said to myself. We were still on the freeway. We had about twenty minutes before arriving downtown. I wasn't the only one coming here for the first time. Half the people on the bus were here for the first time as well. When the Greyhound pulled into the bus station, I started getting nervous. I then proceeded to pray. Then I told myself, "Snap out of this. You have been all over the place. Pull yourself together."

This time things were different. It's not like all of the other trips I'd taken around the world. After getting my bags, I hailed down a taxi to take me to the hotel

"I'll take you to the other side of downtown where hotels are cheaper," the cabbie told me, as I climbed in the backseat.

"Okay, cool."

He took me to 5th and Los Angeles Streets. "It's not the Beverly Inn, but the rooms are nice," he said.

As I stepped out of the cab, I looked at the building across the street and the one I was checking into, and they were the same as the two buildings in my dreams.

"Oh shit," I said, putting my hand over my mouth.

The cab driver asked, "What's wrong?"

"Nothing."

After he took off, I stood on the curb, staring at the two buildings. I could not believe this. Then I looked down the street. I saw people walking around like it was a block party down there.

After checking in, I called Mom. She was going on and on, inquiring about how my trip was going and what part of town I was in.

"Mom, I don't mean to cut you off, but you have to hear this. The hotel that I am staying in and the building across the street are the same two buildings from my dream." I started to walk down that dark road.

"Are you for real?"

"Yes, no joke."

She didn't say a word. Then out of nowhere, she said, "That's déjà vu. You need to pray."

After my thirty-minute conversation with Mom, I returned to my room to put on my hat and jacket. Then I walked outside. My heart was beating fast as I looked down the street. Each block I passed, I saw more and more people. Never in my life have I seen so many homeless people. I could not believe this. My dreams were actually true. All of these people were trapped on the streets of L.A. This road has no ending. It goes on and on.

I went back to my room and lay across the bed, looking at the ceiling. I closed my eyes. "God, what do I do? Why am I here?" I have nothing to give. My life is not much different from theirs. Before I knew it, I dozed off.

I woke up at 8:45 that morning, and by 10:00 a.m. I was out the door. I walked back down that street. It was like a ghost town. There were only a few people in my view. I said, "Wow where did everybody go?" I walked from block to block. The streets were clean, and then I saw a park. As I got closer, I saw a lot of people sleeping everywhere, but only a few people were actually walking and enjoying the park.

I guess the police didn't let them sleep in the park. Everywhere else on the streets was cool. I stayed in the park for a few hours just to see what was going on. A van pulled up and people started running to it. I walked over to the van. The people in the van were giving away food. Out of nowhere, more and more people came running. A fight broke out, the people in the van took off and so did I. *These people are fighting over food like it was the end of the world*, I thought. Wow!

On my way back to the hotel, I saw another van giving food to the homeless. I said, "This must be an everyday thing."

While waiting on the elevator, a lady at the payphone asked if I had change for a dollar. I walked over to her, digging in my pocket for the change.

"Where are you from?"

"What?"

"I know you are not from L.A."

"How do you know that?"

"You have a look about you. I can't place it."

"Oh is that so?" After giving her change, I walked back to the elevator.

"So where are you from?"

"Atlanta."

"Welcome to L.A. Maybe we can hook up later."

"Maybe." I got on the elevator.

"Room 713," she yelled out.

"Okay!" I yelled back.

Inside my room, I started unpacking my things. There was knock at the door. *I didn't tell that girl what room I was in*, I thought. No way had she found me.

"Who is it?" I called out.

It was some woman from across the hall, asking if I had a light, probably just wanting to see who had checked into this room. I opened the door.

"Oh hi, my name is Diamond. I stay in the room across the hall from you. Do you have a light?"

"I'm D." I handed her my lighter. "You you can keep it."

"Where are you from, D?"

Looking perplexed, I said, "Damn, do I look that different than the other Black men around here?"

"Sorry, D, didn't mean to upset you."

I laughed. "I didn't mean it like that." I paused and looked at her. "Somebody in the lobby asked me the same thing. What do I look like, Diamond, what do you see? Please tell me."

"Well, you just have a look about you like you don't belong here. Are you a cop?"

I chuckled. "No, I am not a cop. I just got here from Atlanta."

"Oh okay, D, just be careful. What made you come here?"

"A vision and faith."

She looked at me as she took a drag off her cigarette. "If you want, you can come over later and I can show you around."

"Thanks, but I have to do this on my own. I will stop through sometime though."   She smiled, said, "Okay," and went back inside her room.

They don't waste no time out here, two dates in one hour, I thought, chuckling.

* * *

I started finding my way around downtown L.A. I was getting to know people and places to go just for activity. I started playing ball at the park on 2nd Street where most of the homeless loiter during the day. People were still giving me questionable looks, but I just blocked it out of my mind. On the way back to the hotel, I saw a crowd of people standing on the corner.

"What's going on?" I asked to no one in particular.

"We're waiting for the bus to pick us up and take us to a shelter to get some clothes and food. We'll be spending the night there, too."

"Can anybody go?"

"Yes, the bus will be here in fifteen minutes."

"Okay, thanks."

I didn't have time to go back and change my clothes and I really didn't want to go anywhere looking like I did, but something told me to get on that bus so I stayed.

After the bus pulled up, the driver shouted, "No ID no ride." Everyone started holding up their IDs so I did the same.

After departing from downtown L.A., we hit the freeway. I was trying to look at all of the signs so I would know how to get there if I wanted to go on my own. It was about a thirty-minute ride. We pulled up at a building that didn't have a name on it. I could not see the name of the street we were on so after I got off the bus I asked the name of the street.

"146th Street and Western Avenue," the bus driver answered.

I told him thanks then a man came out to open the gate. He told us to get in line and have our IDs ready.

When we entered the building, there were other people there from the neighborhood. They told us to take one bag and one military cot and find ourselves a spot. It was a big open spaced building. The only rooms with doors were the office, the kitchen and the bathrooms. Men, women and children slept next to one another. For dinner, we had beef stew and white bread. Since I don't eat beef stew, I gave mine to the guy next to me and went back to where we were sleeping for the night. I asked one of the workers where I could take a shower. He told me there was no shower, but I could wash up in the bathroom sink. He asked if I had clean clothes and I told him no, and he gave me some.

After washing up and changing my clothes, I went to sleep. About 5:00 a.m., I woke up to people talking and getting up, so I got up also at 6:00 a.m. It was time to eat. The oatmeal was not to my liking so I passed it down the table. "I'll eat when I get back downtown," I said to myself.

While waiting for the bus to pick us up, a man walked in and everyone who worked there was saying good morning to him. I guess he was the boss. He walked around, looking at everybody and then he looked at me. He walked over to me.

"What's your name?" After I told him my name, he said, "My name is Mr. White. I am the boss. I'm looking for a cook. Can you cook?

"Yes."

"Can you start this week?"

"Yes."

He wanted to know if I had somewhere to stay and I told him I was staying in a hotel in downtown L.A. He told me to get my things and bring them back with me that he had a place for me to stay.

I couldn't believe it, a job and a place to stay. I shook Mr. White's hand. "Thank you, Mr. White."

After getting my things and checking out of the hotel, I took a cab back to the center. Mr. White took me on the other side of the building.

"This is your room. The bathroom and the shower are two doors down. After you finish unpacking, come to my office so you can meet everyone and do some paper work."

After meeting everyone and finishing my paper work, Mr. White took me to the kitchen. The other cook's name was Mike, and this was his last week at the center. He had another job starting next week.

The rest of the week Mike was showing me how to use big pots and make enough food for everyone. I didn't like the way he cooked. He just threw stuff together to make a meal; he never really put any thought into it. After Mike's last day on the job, I changed everything. The kitchen belonged to me.

The co-workers were coming to the kitchen wanting to know what smelled so good. "This kitchen never smelled like this before," one of them said.

"D, I don't care what you are cooking, I want a plate before the bus gets here," another said.

I started laughing. "Okay, I'll hook everybody up."

My first day I cooked baked chicken, greens, cornbread, gravy, yams and rice. After the doors opened to feed the needy, there were about thirty-five people so we had enough food for everybody who wanted a second helping. Between the people and the co-workers, all the food was eaten. I made enough food to feed about eighty people.

After dinner, everyone thanked me for the meal I'd cooked, saying it was the best meal they'd had in a long time. The following day, more people came to the center for dinner. By the end of the week, we had over one hundred people coming for meals. I was astonished, wondering where all these people came from. I found out that the word on the street was the shelter on 146th and Western had a new cook and the best food out of all the shelters. With more and more people coming for meals, I started using people that came to the shelter to help me in the kitchen.

I had five people to help me during dinner service. Before long, people were calling me Brother D.

Mr. White would always come in the kitchen with a big smile on his face, saying, "You are doing a good job. Everybody loves your cooking; so many more people are coming here. Not everyone puts love in their cooking. Keep up the good work, Brother D."

"I will."

At first, I really believed that he cared about the needy, but as time went on, I found out he was only happy because of all the people that were now coming to the shelter. The more people the more money and supplies he received from the government.

After a few months, things in the shelter started to change. Supplies started coming up missing. Mr. White's friends and family started hanging around more. The list of things to give to the needy was getting shorter and shorter. I didn't like what was going on. Since I was the one in charge of the supplies and the only one with a key, I started giving the people what they needed at night, which were clothes. We were getting over one hundred people a night now and we had more than enough to give so that's what I did.

Mike, a co-worker, came to me saying, "Mr. White is going to be mad when he comes in the morning."

"This stuff is for the needy not for his family and friends. Let him be mad."

I had no fear of losing my job if he let me go. The number of people who came here would drop back down to thirty or forty a night, and I know he doesn't want that.

The next morning about 10:30 a.m., I was getting things ready for dinner. I was also ready for Mr. White to walk into the kitchen talking shit. After noon hit, I said to myself, "I know he's here. I heard him talking, but he didn't come into the kitchen." At 5:00 p.m., Mr. White went home and didn't say a word to me all day. That wasn't like him. He cried about everything. So for the rest of the night, I just blocked it out of my head and did my job.

After dinner, I asked Mike where were the clothes for the people who needed them.

"Over there on the table."

"Where are the blankets and sleeping bags?"

"They didn't put any out for the night."

After checking what Mr. White had told Mike to put out for the night, there were only enough things for ten people and we had about twenty-five newcomers at the shelter that night. I went outside to the storage room to get more things. That's when I found out that Mr. White had changed the lock on the storage room door. Damn! That's why he didn't come talking shit to me.

It hurt me to tell them that that was all we had for the night. Some of these people really needed to change clothes tonight. I was really pissed off so I just went to my room to cool off. The following morning I had made up my mind that Mr. White and I would have to have a talk. It was 10:00 a.m. and no Mr. White. It was noon and still no Mr. White. At 2:00 p.m. I went to the office asking Ms. Millie, the person in charge, why Mr. White was not around.

"Where is Mr. White, is he coming in today?"

"Mr. White is out of town for the rest of the month."

"Are you for real?"

"Yes."

"Who has the key to the storage room?"

"I do and Mr. White gave me a list of the things to take out every day."

"You can't go by that list. Some nights we get more women and kids than men. Some nights we get twenty to twenty-five new people. What you had Mike put out last night wasn't enough. Fifteen people walked out of here this morning with the same damn clothes on and five new people that slept on the streets needed a blanket and sleeping bag."

"Well, Mr. White said you were giving out too many supplies."

"That's a damn lie! I only give out what they need. I think you people keep forgetting we don't get twenty to thirty people now, we get over one hundred people every damn night now. Two damn buses and walk-ins." I walked out of the office and went back into the kitchen.

An hour later, Ms. Millie came from the office. "Brother D, come with me to the storage room." She told me to get what I needed. When we got there most of the things were gone. No blankets, no sleeping bags, only a few clothes

"What happened to all of the stuff? I was just in here the other day."

"Mr. White's family came with a truck and took some of the stuff. Mr. White told me they were coming and to let them get what they needed."

"Needed for what?"

"Well, he said they were giving stuff to the needy."

Bullshit, they are not giving stuff to the needy, they are taking that stuff home, I thought.

I told Mike to get the last four bags of clothes and the rest of the canned food for the kitchen.

"It's not my fault, Brother D. I was only following orders," Ms. Millie said.

"I know, but this stuff belongs to the needy, not the people who have big houses, incomes over $50,000 a year and drive new damn cars all of the time."

"I know," she said.

"When is the next shipment coming in?"

"On the thirtieth of this month and that will be the last one for the winter program."

"That's right winter will be over in one month."

I knew that I had to beat Mr. White's family from taking things when the next shipment was brought in. I didn't care about losing my job anymore, I was quitting anyway. One thing I can't stand is fake ass people who act as if they care and steal from the people who are really in need.

Time flew and the end of the month arrived. I heard the truck pull up so I walked outside. After they finished unloading the truck I did what I always do, which was to stock up the kitchen with the meat and canned goods. This time, I intentionally overstocked the kitchen and then took most of the blankets, sleeping bags and clothes to a different spot where no one would find them.

Ms. Millie knew what I was doing, but she didn't interfere. "I don't know nothing," she said, walking back to her office. It was 8:30 p.m.

Suddenly, Mr. White popped up. This was the first time he'd showed up after 5:00 p.m. since I'd been working there. I thought Ms. Millie or Mike must have dropped a dime on me. As I was serving the people, Mr. White walked right into the kitchen. He didn't say "Hello" or anything else to me. He started searching the cabinets. He asked me why I had so much food in there. I told him because last month someone had taken what I needed and for the last week I had to serve soup with no meat in it. So this month I'm making sure that I don't run out of food. "Is that okay with you sir?" He just looked at me; he kept whatever he was thinking to himself.

* * *

It was the last night of the winter program. Some of the people were looking so sad; they were very upset because now they would have to go back to sleeping on the streets. I did what I could to make everybody happy. It wasn't easy when you had over one hundred people depending on you for their dinner. I told everyone to line up. I made four chocolate cakes, and even the co-workers were in the line. People were thanking me for a great last meal. The following morning, I distributed the clothes, blankets and sleeping bags to the people who needed them. After that, I went to my room to rest and to think about what was next.

The following morning I jumped out of bed, thinking I had to cook but then it came to me that the winter program ended the night before. I walked to the store on the next block to get a newspaper. I was looking for a room to rent. I saved most of my money and I knew that Mr. White was going to kick me out soon. I didn't plan on going back to downtown L.A. to stay in a motel. I found a place to stay. It was a nice house with four bedrooms, two bathrooms and the rooms were only $250.00 per month. There were ten people in the house, including myself (both men and women).

After Ms. Moore showed me around the house and introduced me to everyone, I went to my room to unpack my things. I had two roommates: Tony and Pat. We were lucky to have only three people in our room. The other rooms housed four people.

After Ms. Moore left, Pat came into the room, and we talked for a few hours. She was down to earth. I like that in a woman, keeping it real.

* * *

A few weeks later, I went to the EDD office to look for a job. The lady I talked to took me in her office and asked me what line of work I was interested in, and I told her about the winter program.

After she made one phone call, she told me that she might have a job for me. She gave me an address and a phone number and told me they were expecting me that day. She then gave me her card and told me to keep in touch with her. I thanked her and left.

The job I was going to apply for was a cooking position at a center for women. After finding the center, I checked in at the front desk. There were four other people applying for the job. I was the last to be called in an hour later.

As I sat in her office, Ms. Cane looked over my resume. "They call you Brother D?"

"Yes." How do you know that?"

From your resume, it says you cooked for the winter program on Western Avenue."

"Yes, that's right."

"Well, we have a winter program also and this past winter a lot of people were talking about you."

"For real?"

"Yes, they were talking about how good your food was."

"Oh..."

"Why are you looking for another job?"

I didn't tell Ms. Cane the truth. Instead, I told her, "Full-time went to part-time until next winter and I need more than twenty hours a week."

"Brother D, you have the job. I would love for you to cook for our center. From what I've been hearing about your cooking, everyone would love to have you as our new cook."

I thanked Ms. Cane thank, and after leaving I spotted a pay phone that I used to call Ms. Washington from EDD. I told her the good news and thanked her again. "Lunch is on me on Friday. I don't start work until next week."

"Okay," she said.

* * *

After I picked up Ms. Washington for lunch we talked a bit about ourselves.

"Would you mind helping me move some things in my house this weekend?"

"For what you've done for me, how could I say no?" I said.

From that day on, Ms. Washington donned me as her godson. She had two sons of her own. She told me that I was the son that would help her get things done around her house since I knew how to fix everything. Not everyone will take you into their home and make you a part of their family. This was a special day for me. It was my first L.A. family. I stayed for the weekend helping Ms. Washington. She took me home on Sunday evening. She kept trying to pay me for helping her. I wouldn't accept her money

"I have my own money," I told her.

"You can never have too much money so take it."

So I did.

The following Monday I started my new job. The kitchen was bigger, the pay was better, and everything was good. I had to cook for fifty people a day. To me that was a walk in the park.

The women in the program were acting like they had never seen a man before. I won't lie; it felt good getting all of that attention. After working there for a few months, I learned that I had a secret admirer. One of the ladies in the program came into the kitchen while I was cleaning.

"Brother D, I have something for you. It's a letter, but it isn't from me," she said.

The letter had no name on it, but the person who wrote it stated that they were in love with me and wanted to have my baby when they got out of the program. *This must be a joke*, I thought. I put the letter in my pocket and went home laughing.

The following day, the lady who gave me the letter kept watching me while I was in the break room. I asked her who had given her the letter.

"I can't tell you that, she would be very upset."

"Can you give me a hint?"

"Okay, look around when you serve us lunch and see who keeps looking at you the whole time and not eating."

"Okay cool, thanks Kenyalle."

Twelve noon came and it was time to feed the ladies. I did what Kenyalle told me to do, but damn there were about ten ladies looking at me and not eating. I laughed out loud. I tried all week to find out who it was. It was driving me crazy. Then out of nowhere, a girl came into the kitchen while I was turning the lights off. Her name was LaKendra.

"Hi, Brother D!"

"What are you doing in here?"

"I was just about to lock the kitchen."

"I can't fight it anymore."

"Fight what?"

"I love you, I want you."

Oh my, God. It's my secret admirer, I thought. "But LaKendra, you don't really know me. How can your feelings be so deep?"

"You don't believe in love at first sight?"

"You've never felt that before?"

"Not really."

"Well, I have and it was with you."

"How long had she been in the program?"

"Four months, but we get to go out every other weekend and next weekend is my day out. I want to spend it with you. I will pay for everything, the room, the food everything just don't tell me no."

"Wow, you have it all planned out. Don't you think you are moving a little too fast? We don't even know each other, and you're talking about a room. Let's get to know each other first."

"Yeah, you're right."

"Well, I'm going home now. I will let you know before the week is out if we can hook up Saturday." She asked me for a hug as I was walking out of the kitchen. I stopped in my tracks then turned around and said, "Why not?"

As the week went by, LaKendra was passing me letter after letter. It was driving me crazy. I didn't know how to tell her that we could not get together on Saturday without hurting her feelings. She was a very nice girl, but she was in the program for a reason. What that reason was I didn't know. The staff is not allowed to give out people's personal information. Friday evening I had to tell this girl something. After lunch, I told LaKendra I would meet her at the address she had given me, which was her sister's house. I told her I'd be there at 8:30 p.m. She just smiled and gave me a hug.

* * *

Saturday at 8:15 p.m., I took a cab to LaKendra's sister's house and I was nervous. She saw me get out the cab. She was standing by the front gate.

After going inside, I asked, "Where is your sister?"

"They went out; she gave me the house for a few hours."

"Well, that was nice of her."

She asked what I had in the bag I told her it was some wine. I asked her if she could drink wine.

"Tonight, I can drink and do what I want to do." We both laughed.

We got comfortable on the couch and talked while we listened to some music. About 10:30 p.m., I told her it was time for me to go and asked if she would call me a cab. After she hung up the phone, she said the cab would be there in about an hour.

While waiting on the cab, I had another drink of wine. LaKendra started feeling on my chest. I told her that it was not a good idea to get a man all worked up on the first date. She started laughing and said, "You're different from other men."

"Well, I respect myself as well as I respect you."

"If you have deep feelings for a person you don't want to give them the cookies in the jar on the first date, now do you?"

"D, I only have two months left in the program. I really like you. Will you still see me after I'm out?"

"LaKendra, when you get out your feelings won't be as strong as they are now. You only feel like this because you see me every day."

"Plus, I am the only man in the building."

"No, you're wrong. Time will tell the truth."

The cab was outside blowing. I gave LaKendra a kiss and a hug. She smiled as I walked out of the door.

Two months had passed, and LaKendra was gone. I have never heard from her or seen her since.

* * *

It was winter again, and it was time to feed the needy and take in the homeless. On the first night of the winter program, we had ten walk-ins and twenty-five more that came by bus. As I was serving the food, I heard someone call my name. It was Janet. She used to come by the shelter where I cooked last winter. We talked for a minute.

"A lot of people went to the shelter where you used to work. They're going to be very upset when they find out you are not there."

I laughed and said, "Well, tell them where I am." She said she would.

The next day we had twenty-five walk-ins and a full bus. I had to make more food. I was hearing my name all over the place. It was like old times for the rest of the winter. More and more people started showing up. I had grown attached to not some, but all the people who walked through that door. I thought I had heard it all before. I started working with the homeless. After getting to know most of them and them getting to know me, some of the stories told were unbelievable.

About thirty-five percent of the people on the streets today had good jobs, nice homes, and they didn't lose what they had because of drugs or alcohol. Some of the people I knew lost everything because of stress, depression, divorce, etc. Some had even tried suicide to escape from reality. I saw old IDs that confirmed that at one time or another these people were doctors, teachers and the list goes on. I asked a few of them if they had faith in God and they told me no. I knew that without faith failure was the only option. Faith and vision was what got me here.

Chapter 2

During the summer, my boss told me she would have to cut my hours because most of the women were done with their rehabilitation.

Winter is a long way from now. So my hours were cut in half from forty a week to twenty a week. There was no way in the world I could live off that little bit of money. I knew it was time for me to move on. After getting home, there was a letter from some senior citizens center telling me to call if I couldn't make my interview on next Tuesday. What interview? I hadn't applied for any job working with senior citizens. I didn't even know where the place was located.

The next day at work, I called the senior citizens center.

"Are you sure you have the right person?"

"Yes. So Mr. Barnes you will be here Tuesday, right?

"What time?"

"Nine a.m."

"I will be there."

I was very puzzled for the rest of the day. I called my friend Ms. Washington who worked for the EDD office. I asked her if she had put the application in for me at the senior citizens center.

"No, I thought you were still working at the women's center."

I told her I was and I told her about the cut in my hours. When I told her I was going on the interview on Tuesday, she wished me good luck.

The following Tuesday at the center for seniors I was told to have a seat, but I was dying to see my application so I went up to the front desk.

"May I please see my application?"

"Just a minute, I just had it in my hand. I don't know what happened to it. Well Mr. Barnes do you mind filling out another one?"

"No problem."

Before I could complete the application, I was called in for my interview. I walked into the office of Mr. David Green where there were five people seated around his desk. I was met with "Pleased to meet you" and handshakes from all.

Did I hit the lotto or something? Mr. Green told me the job was mine if I wanted it and that I would be driving a company car delivering meals to senior citizens—eight hours a day, five days a week and with weekends off.

"I'll take it!"

"You're hired. This is Mr. Lee, your supervisor. He will show you around and get you started come next Monday.

"Thank you, Mr. Green. Have a nice day."

Mr. Lee showed me around the center, we talked for a few minutes, and then I went home. I walked down the street to the store on my way to the bus stop. When I got to the bus stop, a lady handed me a magazine. I knew she was a Jehovah's Witness; they were all over the place. The front cover read: *Do you know the power of God?*

After reading a few pages, my mind was clear on all that had been going on since I'd arrived in Los Angeles. This was a task, I was a servant, I was walking blind but He was guiding me. I did not pick those jobs He did. The who, what, when, where and how were no more. I was starting to see things more clearly.

* * *

Monday morning at 7:00 a.m. I was on the job. After meeting everyone, Mr. Lee and I started loading the car with one hundred twenty meals. It was a lot of food to deliver in eight hours.

"It's not as bad as it looks," Mr. Lee said. "Some drivers get it done in six hours. When you get used to your route, it will be a piece of cake."

We were almost done by 3:00 p.m. Once we returned to the center, Mr. Lee informed me that on Wednesday I would be in my second day of training. I was on my own.

Tuesday morning was my turn to drive and deliver all the meals. Some of the people on my route were bedridden. Taking them their meals and seeing them was heartbreaking. Some liked to talk because they had no one around to talk to, and some were afraid to open the door so we left their meals on the front porch. Some asked for extra meals because this was the only meal they received in a day and they had no extra money to buy themselves food. Once their bills were paid, they were broke.

By the end of the day, I wasn't feeling so good. It was hard to see so many people who had no help. After getting home, I went into my room to lay down. I started thinking whether or not this was the right job for me. Then something came into my head, telling me to stay strong. I knew that it was God telling me that.

After a few weeks I had my route down pat, but I was still feeling the pain of some of those people. I informed my supervisor of some of the problems they were having and all I got from him was "Don't worry about it."

"How can I not worry about it? I see these people every day?" Then I walked away.

By the end of the month, I had more and more people reaching out for help. When I returned to the center, everyone was in the break room. I had forgotten about the Driver of the Month award. As I sat down, my name was called.

"Well Mr. Barnes, are you coming up here to get your money and your award or do you want for me to keep it?" asked Mr. Barnes.

Everyone laughed.

"No, I'm coming. This is a big surprise for me."

"Your car was very clean every day, on time in the mornings, good reports from the people on your route and a good report from your supervisor. Keep up the good work."

"Thank you."

I got home feeling good about my award I took the fifty dollars and went out to eat.

The next four months in a row, I won the Driver of the Month award, which brought on a lot of hate and jealousy from other employees. Not only was I having problems with co-workers, I was also having problems with some of the people on my route. I had ten people who needed someone to help them, and there was no way I could tell them no. So every day after work, I would go to the store for them, pay some bills for them and help around their house. Seven out of ten had family near, but they would not pitch in and do anything to help. It's pretty sad when you have a house full of people and you have to bring someone from the outside to get things done.

By the sixth month, I was still winning the Driver of the Month award. Also during this time, helping ten people went up to twenty people. I had saved enough money to buy a car. Now I was able to help five more people a day and get things done faster. I was not getting enough rest; by the time I made it home I didn't have long to sleep. I would get in bed and close my eyes, but my brain would not turn off. All the hate I was getting from my co-workers, plus all the people on my route who needed help, kept me in a fog.

I decided I was going to do my very best not to win the Driver of the Month award next month. That would take some of the heat off me from the haters on my job. By the middle of the month, a position for field case manager was open. If I could land that position, I would be able to help a lot more of the seniors. I had perfect attendance, I received Driver of the Month for the last six months in a row; it was time for someone to move up in this department, so I went to the main office and put in an application for the position.

The next day on my route, I told everyone about the good news. They were all praying that I would get the position. It would be two months before they made the choice for the position known to the employees. I wasn't getting any sleep as it was, and now I knew I wasn't really going to sleep well. I was so anxious about whether I would be their choice for the position I'd applied for. The next morning, a new driver was starting. I found out he used to work there before so he didn't need any training. His name was Dan. One week later, Dan didn't show up for work nor did he call. So his route was split between me and two other drivers, but we still had to get it done in eight hours and there was no overtime.

Dan had done this three times in one month and gotten away with it. The following month during the Driver of the Month award ceremony, Ms. Smith called Dan's name as the Driver of the Month. Not only was I shocked, all the other drivers and co-workers were also. Everybody looked at each other, as if to say, "This must be a joke." I didn't ask Ms. Smith how in the hell Dan had won Driver of the Month. I was just glad I had not won again.

A few weeks later while giving Ms. Williams her meal, she wasn't looking so good. I asked her what was wrong. She told me that she was tired of people taking from her and using her and these people were her own children. She showed me a water bill and a light bill that totaled of $900.00.

"D, I give my son enough money every month to pay all of the bills. He's not paying them. I don't have anyone I can trust."

"Do you have a checking account?"

"Yes."

"When I get off work at three o'clock, be ready. I'll be back to pick you up."

After work, I had to call a few seniors to let them know that I would not be able to make it that day. While parking my car in front of Ms. Williams' house her son was coming out of her front door. He saw me, but didn't say a word. He just took off down the street. I went inside to get Sister Williams. I took her to the bank to set up an account where her bills could be paid from automatically. The bank told us it would be a few days before things went into effect. She no longer had to worry about paying her bills. She thanked me and I took her back home.

* * *

As time progressed, my five-day-a-week job turned into a seven-day-a-week job. Some of the people on my route had lost their weekend help due to cutbacks on their income so they had no one to feed them on the weekends. I told them I would come by on Saturdays and Sundays to bring them food. I had about fifteen people that I did this for every weekend, but I really didn't mind. I was thankful that I was able to be of help. By the end of the month, there was a lot going on. I had to pick up donations, "Driver of the Month" and field case manager position. For some reason, everyone on my route was giving more than usual at the end of each month. They gave me hugs and said, "God is going to bless you." I told them He already has.

After making it back to the center (this was the first time I had to use a trash bag to hold the donations), Mr. Lee and Ms. Smith were in the lobby waiting for everyone to return and asked me what was in the bag. I turned the bag upside down and money and checks went all over the table. Their eyes got big.

There was over nine hundred dollars' worth of donations in that trash bag. That was the first time that much money had ever been donated at once. The next day after work, it was time for the "Driver of the Month" award. They called someone new. His name was Gonzalez. He was even shocked to hear his name called. Everyone thought that since I had come in with that large donation amount I would win again. One thing they don't know about me, I don't do things for a reward. After the "Driver of the Month" ceremony, I went home.

I didn't have to help anyone today. I spent a few hours cleaning, which was something that was past due. The next morning at work a new driver was starting. I asked whose place he was taking. Mr. Lee said, "Dan's." *I knew he wasn't going to make it. He was always late, didn't clean his car and stayed on the phone*, I thought. Even after he brought his kids to work with him they still gave him the "Driver of the Month" award. I had to laugh out loud.

After I was done with my route, I pulled up into the center and saw Dan unloading his car, taking things into the field case manager's office.

"Dan what are you doing?"

"Moving into my office."

"Your office?"

"Yeah, I'm the new field case manager. That's why you didn't see me this morning."

My heart broke into a million pieces. I was at a loss for words. I got back into my car and went home. I turned my phoned off. I didn't want to see or talk to anyone for the rest of the day. This was the first time in my life that I used every curse word in the book.

I took my anchor off the wall. After seeing all the holes I'd made with my fist, I felt a lot better. The next morning at work, the other drivers were saying what I was saying. How in the hell did Dan get that position? He had only been there for three and half months. Everyone knew I was the one for that spot. After loading my car with the meals for the seniors, I went looking for Mr. Lee. He was nowhere to be found. I didn't even see his car in the parking lot. I took off on my route. I was telling everyone what had happened. I had no idea that someone would call in and ask why I didn't get the field case manager position. Now everyone in the office hated on me.

Mr. Lee must not have been able to face me; it had been three days and I had not seen him. On the fourth day, at 7:00 a.m., Mr. Lee was in the kitchen. I walked up to him and asked him how someone with poor attendance, who'd been written up on two occasions and was always late, got to be a field case manager. Mr. Lee could not even look up at me, let alone give me an answer. I just turned and walked away.

After I finished my route, I went to the main office and asked if I could see Mr. David Green. Ms. Moore at the front desk told me to have a seat. Fifteen minutes later, I was able to see Mr. Green. After pleading my case, Mr. Green said he had been receiving bad reports about me from Mr. Lee. I couldn't believe what he said.

"You have to be joking. Tell me you are joking."

"No, it's the truth."

"I was Driver of the Month six months in a row. I have never missed a day of work in eight months. I came in last month with $900.00 in donations. I have perfect attendance. Mr. Lee must have me mixed up with Dan. He is the one that's been getting written up every month, not me."

Mr. Green said he would look into it. I wasn't going to hold my breath. I can look in a man's eyes and see the truth. When I walked out of his office, I knew it would be the last time I'd see Mr. Green. After that day, I was getting a lot of hate from people on the job—my co-workers, supervisors, even from the main office. So I just stayed to myself and did my job.

People on my route were still calling and complaining about why I hadn't been chosen for the case manager's position. They had no idea what I was up against every morning when I walked into that center. After a year, it was time for me to take my vacation. I got one week off. I told the seniors who depended on me for food on the weekends that I would still be taking care of them while I was off. I looked for a new job, but I didn't have any luck. The following week I returned to work, but I didn't feel like I used to feel about my job. I didn't care about anything that was going on there anymore.

Moving up, becoming the Driver of the Month; it was all dead in my mind. The only care I had was for the people on my route. How could I tell that it was time for me to move on? A few weeks later, while delivering meals, I got a phone call from Mr. Manuel. He used to be on my route. He asked me to stop by and to let him know what day I'd be coming because someone wanted to meet with me.

During my lunch hour, I stopped at the store to get a newspaper to see if there was job in there, but still I had no luck. All the jobs I called about had already been filled. "God, where do I go from here?" After getting off work and helping a few people on my route, I took a ride to the beach, just to relax my brain. After a few hours, I went home.

The next day on my route, Mr. Manuel called me again, asking, "Are you coming today?" I told him yes, that I would be there when I finished working around 4:30 p.m. I had to take care of something else first. I had promised Ms. Gale that I would take her to the store when I got off. While taking Ms. Moore her meal, she came to the door asking if I could pick up a few things from the store for her. After getting off work, Ms. Gale and I were in the store and my phone started ringing off the hook. For some reason it seemed like everyone needed something. What's going on today? After I took Ms. Gale home and made six more drop offs it was 5:30 p.m. I called Mr. Manuel to ask if it was too late for me to come by, he told me it was not too late.

When I got to Mr. Manuel's house, I met his sister, Ms. Gonzalez. She asked me if I knew someone that could do in-home care from 8:00 a.m. to 4:00 p.m. Monday through Friday. I told her to give me a few days and I would let her know.

After getting home, I thought about Ms. Gonzalez, and realized I didn't need to look for another job. There was one right under my nose. The next day I called Ms. Gonzalez and told her I would take the job, but I needed thirty days before I could start, and she agreed. After getting to Ms. Gibson's house and dropping off her meal, she asked if I knew someone that did in-home care. I laughed.

"Did I say something funny?" she asked.

"No, it's just that Mr. Manuel's sister asked me the same thing not long ago."

Once I started looking for a job, people on my route started popping up in need of home care.

After thirty days, I quit my job. Everyone on my route knew I was leaving a week before my last day. There were so many tears and hugs. No one wanted to see me leave, but everyone on my route knew the hell I was going through on that job. After telling them I would still be around, most of them were so happy to hear that I started working with Mr. Manuel and Ms. Gibson during the week and would still be able to keep bringing food on the weekends to the people from my old job. I would also still be able to take them to the store when I had the time.

Some of the people from my old job had become family. I took them under my wing and they took me under theirs. The only sad thing about caring and loving someone, especially the elderly, is sooner or later the Lord calls them home. After a few years, I started losing my family and friends. My phone was not ringing off the hook like it used to anymore. I started seeing "for sale" signs in the yards of some of the people I knew. When I didn't hear from certain people, I would call or go by their homes.

Some were in the hospital, some were in nursing homes and some of them had passed on to a better life. When Mr. Manuel stopped walking, they transferred him into a nursing home. Ms. Gibson's daughter moved her in with her and just like that no job and most of my friends and family were gone. Out of the one hundred twenty people I had on my route, I had taken responsibility for sixty. When I quit my job, sixty went down to twenty-five. After a few years, it dropped down to five. Out of the five people left, one of them had become my best friend. I used to bring her mom meals, too. Now her mom is in a better place so we both know what it is like to lose someone you love.

I thank God I stayed strong enough to complete the task. It's been quite an experience for me. Love, care, trust, abuse, death, pain, illness, suicides, depression and responsibility. People who knew me always asked me, "Man, how do you do it?" Well you have to have love in your heart, faith and patience. If you have all three and more, you can walk through the valley of the shadow of death and have no fear because you know that He is with you. If you don't know who He is, it's never too late to learn. Read the Bible.

Chapter 3

The Walk, The Task, The Vision

After a few months, I found another job working at the center for the needy. We gave out clothes and food. My boss, Mr. Victor, told me he had to make a run. The lady who worked at the front desk would be here in an hour. I was told to show her around and tell her to start on the files that were on the desk, which would be hers. An hour later, a nice looking sister walked in, and I asked her name. She told me it was Ms. Jackie Hawthorne. I showed her around before taking her to her desk, as my boss had asked.

When I got off work, I saw Ms. Hawthorne walking to the bus stop. I offered her a ride home. During the ride, she wanted to know about me so I gave her a little information about myself and in turn, she gave me a little information about herself. I think she just wanted to know if I was single. I was shocked to hear that she was single, too.

"Stop calling me Ms. Hawthorne. Jackie will do just fine."

"Okay, Ms. Jackie." After dropping Jackie off at home, I went home.

For the rest of the week I was taking Jackie home after work and some days we would sit in the car in front of her house and talk for two to three hours.

One Friday night she said, "I feel like I've known you all of my life and it's only been a week since we've met. I want you to come in and meet my daughter."

After getting in the house, she told me to follow her. She took me to her daughter's room.

"Mae, this is Brother D, Brother D this is Mae, my daughter."

I couldn't believe my eyes. Seeing this child smile while hooked up to so many machines was a miracle. A chill went through my whole body. Jackie walked out of the room and told me to talk to Mae while she went to change her clothes.

For the first time in my life, I didn't know what to say or do. My eyes started to tear up. I said to myself, "Be strong," then I wiped my face and started talking to Mae. Mae was handicapped—physically and mentally. She was blind in one eye, hard of hearing, couldn't walk or talk and was on a feeding tube. This child had everything in the book wrong with her, but still she smiled with such happiness. After Jackie came back into the room, she started to play with Mae and asked her "Do you like Brother D?"

Mae started kicking the wall, and moving all over the place.

"Is she okay, Jackie?"

"She's telling me she likes you. She's never done that before with anyone."

I reached out to touch Mae's hand. She squeezed my hand hard.

"Wow, she's very strong."

"I know. Sometimes when I'm fixing her tubes, she gets me in a headlock."

"Wow," I said in amazement. I played with Mae for a few hours. I just could not take my eyes off her.

After I got home, I could not hold it in anymore. Never in my life had I seen a child like her before. Not only was she a miracle child she was a special child. I tried to go to sleep, but my brain wouldn't turn off. All I was seeing was Mae.

It wasn't long before Jackie and I had become the best of friends. I could not go one day without spending some time with Mae. She had become my world. I asked Jackie what happened with Mae's dad.

"He took off when Mae started getting sick. He didn't want any part of a handicapped child."

"He's going to pay for that."

I started playing a part in taking care of Mae. Jackie showed me how to work the machines, how much medicine to give her and what to look for when she had pains. It was a lot of work. Mae had two nurses, but some nights Jackie had to play nurse. Sometimes she would be burned out and ask if I could watch Mae for her. I was always pleased to help; she needed to rest.

Mae didn't sleep much. Some nights she didn't fall asleep until three or four in the morning, but it didn't bother me. I would watch television and check on her every fifteen to twenty minutes.

Eventually, Jackie and I started dating. She was the sweetest woman I had ever known. Some days she would be so burned out from working and taking care of Mae, I would do things to get her to laugh or just to see her smile.

"That's why my child and I love you so much," she would say to me. "You know when we need cheering up."

January 7 was Mae's birthday and we had a party for her. A few people came over. She was so happy. I wished she could eat food. I knew she wanted a piece of this cake.

After we sung happy birthday to Mae, Jackie took some ice cream, just a little, so Mae could taste it. She started kicking the wall, which was her way of saying, "Give me some more." We started laughing and Jackie gave Mae a little more just to calm her down.

"Mae, you are not a little girl anymore. You are now eight years old," I told her.

Jackie and I showed Mae all the things we got her for her birthday. She had a big smile on her face. I took Mae out of her bed and put her in the wheelchair. I turned on the music and we started dancing. She was so happy. After the party Mae went to sleep; we knew she had enjoyed her birthday. I kissed Mae on her forehead and told her I loved her.

A few weeks later, Mae had gotten sick. She was in and out of the hospital some nights. I would stay with Jackie all night. She would tell me to go home and get some sleep, but I stayed anyway and leave for work the next morning from the hospital. I was not myself on the days Mae was sick. Some nights I would pray, asking God to take the pain from Mae and give it to me. No one but God and I knew how much this child meant to me. You would think I was her biological father. Seeing this child suffer and still smile when she would see me opened my eyes about life. On bad days on the job or just when people said or did things to try and piss me off; being around that child would just take all of that stress away.

I prayed every night that Mae would get better. The doctors were doing everything they could to help Mae, but nothing was working. Mae was transferred to a rehabilitation center. Every day after work, Jackie and I would visit her. After two weeks, Mae was doing a little better. She smiled again when she heard my voice.

"Look, she's smiling," I said to Jackie, but she was so down and burned out from staying up every night and driving back and forth to the center, she just looked up and put her head back down.

After playing with Mae, I talked with Jackie, thinking what I could do to raise her spirits. Her mind was in a whole different world.

She looked up at me. "Did you say something, D?"

"No, I'm talking to myself," I said, which I was.

A month later, Jackie called me at work saying Mae could come home, and that everything was back to normal. Jackie was back to her old self.

A year had come and gone, it was Mae's birthday once again, and she did what she normally did, threw a fit behind the ice cream. Seeing Mae grow up with all that she'd been through and was still going through was a true blessing. My little angel was nine years old now. No one could understand why I put so much time into a child that wasn't mine. I guess you have to know what love is to understand why.

A few months after her ninth birthday, Mae passed away, and my life was not the same. My heart was broken into little pieces. After the funeral, Jackie thanked me for what I'd done for Mae.

"My life with that child was no favor. I loved Mae like she was my flesh and blood. That child was my world and now she's gone. my life will never be the same."

"D, I know you did that's why I'm thanking you. You did more for my child than her own father did and he had the nerve to show up at her funeral like he'd been in her life all of this time."

I didn't want to hear any more about Mae or her father so I just went home. I was already upset. I had just lost the closest thing to my heart.

After a few months, I had a dream about Mae. She was sitting on a bench like she was waiting for something. I told Jackie about the dream.

"She's talking to you. My child really loved you," Jackie replied.

About four months later, I had another dream about Mae. This time she was with another little girl. They were holding hands and waving at me then they walked away. When I woke up, I walked outside, looked up at the sky and said, "She's home now."

Still to this day I think about Mae. My love for her will always be strong. It's sad to say everything you grow to love always come to an end. Jackie and I stayed together for a few more years before she went her way and I went mine.

Chapter 4

———◆◆◆◆◆———

Learning the Life of Muslims

As time moved on not only did I lose my best friend Mae I also lost one of my clients that I worked for doing In Home Supportive Services. Times were getting pretty rough for me. On my way to the gym, I stopped in a Muslim restaurant. This was the first time I stopped in this place and I'd been going to the gym next door for more than two years. I had no idea what made me stop in this time. After checking out the menu, all the food was health food, low calories, so I ordered a veggie burger with green tea. The brother that took my order was the owner of the restaurant. His name was Mohammed.

While waiting on my meal, I started looking in the newspaper for full time work.

"Where are you from?" Brother Mohammed asked me.

I laughed.

"Did I say something funny?"

"No sir, it's just that everybody I meet knows that I'm not from Los Angeles. What do you see that made you asked me that?"

"You just don't look like a Cali."

"That still didn't answer my question. I've been asking people from day one what they see and they all say the same thing." Then I said, "Washington DC"

"Are you for real?"

"Yes."

"I'm from DC."

"Oh my, God!

As we started talking about different parts of DC, I knew he was for real.

Fifteen minutes passed and I was still waiting on my veggie burger. Brother Mohammed just kept on talking and my stomach kept growling. Finally, after twenty minutes, my food was in front of me. While I was eating, Brother Mohammed was telling me he was going to close the shop and move back home. Business was just too slow. I asked him how much he could pay an hour to help get things rolling. I told him the shelters I used to cook for and in my younger days, I cooked for a lot of restaurants.

"Leave me your number. If I forget to call you stop by in three days."

I agreed went next door to the gym.

After getting home, I started thinking what it would be like to work with Muslims. I had only heard about them and all I knew about them was what I saw in the movie *Malcolm X*. I felt this would be a great experience for me. "I hope Brother Mohammed calls," I said to myself. Three days later and there was no call from Brother Mohammed, so when I got off from work, I stopped by the restaurant.

There were two people sitting at the bar waiting for their food and like always Brother Mohammed was talking up a storm.

"Brother Mohammed, how are you doing today?"

He turned around. "Oh how are you doing, Brother D? Have a seat. I'll be right with you." He returned his attention to the two brothers who were waiting on their food. One hour later he called me to the back and started showing me how he did things. I knew from that moment on, I had the job.

I stayed the rest of the evening working with Brother Mohammed. Four hours and only one customer walked through the door and they only wanted a Gensing shot. By 9:00 p.m., Brother Mohammed closed the shop. I told him I could work from the time he opened until 6:00 p.m., five days a week and he agreed. I was still able to keep my part-time job working for In Home Supportive Service. It was only twenty hours a week from 6:00 a.m. to 10:00 a.m. Brother Mohammed's shop didn't open until 12:00 noon, so everything was perfect. The following Monday I started my new job. Brother Mohammed was showing me how to make lunch plates and dinner plates. He told me how slow it was at lunchtime.

"Do you have signs on each corner of the block," I asked him.

"No," he said.

I found some wood in the back and made two signs. Then I asked, "Do you have lunch flyers?"

"Yes, I do," he said, pointing where I can find the flyers.

I took some flyers across the street to the EDD office where my friend Mrs. Washington worked and told her about my new job. I asked her to spread the word to all of her co-workers, and she agreed. I walked all over the neighborhood spreading flyers. It took me hours.

When I got back to the shop there were three men standing by the door talking to Brother Mohammed. As I walked by, one of them said "As'salaam alaikum," but I didn't know what he was saying so I just said, "How are you doing brother?"

"You hired a non-Muslim to work with you?" the man said.

Brother Mohammed looked at me and I looked at him. He told the brother to step outside. I don't know what Brother Mohammed was saying to him because I could not hear them. When Brother Mohammed walked back into the shop, I asked him if there was a problem. He said don't worry about it. He didn't have to tell me. I already knew I was not a Muslim.

After a few weeks, more and more people started coming in for lunch and I had the menu down to perfection. People were getting their food in less than five minutes. Brother Mohammed just moved out of the kitchen when he saw how fast I was moving. Also more Muslims started coming in to eat. As days turned to weeks and weeks turned to months I was now a part of the Muslim family. While I was making lunch for my little buddies—Mary, Patti, Jaden and Nick—I noticed a Muslim lady staring at me. She came in the same time every day and only ordered a glass of water.

After I gave the kids their veggie burgers, I went over with a glass of water before she asked for it. "Here's your glass of water, madam. Would you like a lemon with a straw?" I was acting like a waiter in a Beverly Hills restaurant. She started laughing and so did the kids. I asked the sister her name. She told me Ahlam. It means witty one who has pleasant dreams.

While waiting on the kid's mom to come back and pick them up....yes I was a babysitter too...Ahlam and I sparked a conversation. She had a very pretty face, and that was all I could see as her whole body was covered. That's how Muslim women dress. She asked me if the four kids were mime and I said that's only half of them, the other four were with their mom. I tried to keep a straight face, but when she started choking on her water I started laughing. We sat and talked while my little buddies and their mom went next door to work out for an hour.

"Brother D, you are a funny man."

"When you come here, why do you only order a glass of water?"

"I eat before I come here and I like to watch you cook. I have never seen anyone that can make five to six orders at one time. Brother Mohammed takes twenty minutes to make one order."

We laughed.

"Yeah I know."

"Are you married?"

"Not yet, hope to be one day."

"Do you have a girlfriend?"

"Why all of the questions?"

"Brother D, I like you. If I give you my number, will you call me?"

"Hmmmmm…let me ask the kids."

She stopped me from asking the kids by putting her hand over my mouth.

I chuckled. "Okay, okay you win. I'll call you."

She smiled and walked out of the door. Sister Ahlam was going to school to become a nurse.

After getting home and relaxing my feet, I called Ahlam. She did not answer the phone, but her mother did. She told me that Ahlam was still in school so I gave her my name and number and waited for Ahlam to call me. She hadn't called by 10:30 that night so I went to bed.

The next day at 2:30, Sister Ahlam entered the restaurant.

"As'salaam alaikum, Brother D."

"Waalaikum as'salaam, Sister Ahlam. Have a seat I'll get your water."

"I'll take the lunch special with that glass of water.

"What? Someone didn't eat at home today?"

"I think it's time to try your food to see who's going to be doing the cooking."

I turned from the stove and faced her. "What was that?"

She was laughing up a storm. After making her lunch, I had time to kill.

"Did you get the message I gave your mom last night?"

"Yes, but I got home too late. She told me this morning."

"Now you have my number."

"I don't have school tonight, so I'll give you a call."

"Okay." I smiled.

As we were talking, a customer walked in so I had to get back to work. Sister Ahlam was done with her lunch so she took off.

After a couple months of talking, we were going on our first date. After getting to her house I saw three ladies standing outside.

"Excuse me ladies can you tell Sister Ahlam that Brother D is here?"

They started laughing.

"What's so funny?"

"Brother D it's me…Ahlam."

I couldn't believe my eyes. This was the first time I had seen her in regular clothes and with hair on her head. I looked up in the sky and said, "God forgive me, but *damn* this sister is fine."

Inside the car, she said, "So Brother D what do you think?"

"About what?"

"Now that you have seen the real me, what do you think?"

"You are okay."

She gave me a look like she wanted to take my head off. "Okay?" she said, hitting my arm. "What do you mean okay?"

I started laughing and then I looked her right in her eyes. "You are beautiful." I kissed her on the cheek. She looked at me with a smile.

After dinner and a movie, we went to my place. This was the first time Sister Ahlam had been to my place. I turned on the radio.

"You have to forgive me, I don't have any Muslim music." We laughed.

Around 1:00 a.m., I took Sister Ahlam home. She wasn't ready to leave but I didn't want one thing to lead to another. I respected her too much to let that happen. She wasn't like all the rest of the women I had dated. I knew if I took it to the next level, I was going to have to marry this woman. She wasn't going to let me hit it then quit it. Not to say that I would have done something like that, but I knew what she wanted and I wasn't sure if it was what I wanted, too. We did kiss a few times and played around, but that was it. Sometimes it pays to think with the head on your shoulders...

As time went on, Sister Ahlam kept asking me if I was ready to go to the next level. I kept saying no. She was very upset with me.

For the next few weeks, Ahlam wasn't calling me or coming by the shop. So one day when I got off work I stopped by her house. She was at home and I asked if I could talk to her for a few minutes.

She looked at me. "Why?"

"Please, Ahlam, just a few minutes."

She walked with me to the car.

"Ahlam, you are a Muslim and I am not. I don't think I'll ever be one and I know that if we take this to the next level something is going to have to give. I am not willing to become something that I'm not. I have deep feelings for you, God knows I do, so don't hate me. You should be thanking me for not taking advantage of you and then dumping you like a bad piece of meat. I want us to still be good friends."

She looked at me. "Brother D, I'm not going anywhere."

As time moved on, Brother Mohammed was telling me that the next week would be the ninth month of Ramadan. "We go from sun up to sundown, fasting and towards the end of Ramadan Muslims celebrate the festival of fast breaking," he said.

"But July is not the ninth month."

"It is on our calendar."

The following week there was not one Muslim to walk into the shop, just our regular everyday customers. I was also fasting. The first day for me was not easy. Working with food while my stomach talked to me was a big challenge.

Around 7:30 p.m., the sun started going down, and I was so happy. I could eat a whole bucket of chicken all by myself right now. After the sun set, people started coming in so I had to stop eating and start cooking. The last two hours before closing made up for the slow day we'd had. It went on like this until the last day of Ramadan. Brother Mohammed told me on the last day that all the Muslims go to different Muslim restaurants to eat. Out of all of the years I'd been working here, they never came here to eat.

"But why not?"

"I don't know."

So during my break I went next door to the Masjid to talk with a few Muslims. I was doing what I could to get them to spread the word. I even put more signs out on the streets. Then I called a few of my friends to come down to the restaurant and just chill. I told them I might need them to work that night. I had a good feeling we were going to get hit with a big crowd of Muslim customers.

About 6:30 p.m. that evening, it was as dead as a doorknob. Michelle and Susie were about to go home. I asked them to give me one more hour

"They're not coming," Brother Mohammed said and went upstairs.

Everybody was giving up, but I had this feeling that they were going to come. At 7:30 p.m., five Muslims walked into the shop and then seven more.

I yelled upstairs to Brother Mohammed. "Get down here. I need you."

I was trying to get everybody in place. As more and more people walked through the door, a line started to form outside.

Michelle and Susie were taking orders and Brother Mohammed was trying to help me cook, but he was just in my way, so I put him on the cash register.

Then I told Michelle to call her sister and her cousin and tell them to fly over here because we needed more help. From 7:30 p.m. to 11:00p.m., we worked like dogs chasing cats. After cooking for the last customer, I went in the bathroom to wash my face. I looked in the mirror. My face was so black you would think I had come out of a coal mine. By 1:00 a.m., it was time to go home. Brother Mohammed made more money in a few hours than he had ever made in a year.

He gave everybody an extra $25.00 for helping. I was looking for a bonus check, but all I got was a "Thank you." I was too tired to argue so I told the girls "Thank you for helping" and just went home.

After Ramadan, more and more Muslims were walking through the door. So Brother Mohammed hired a waitress named Gloria. She was cool; she just talked too much. Some days it felt like my ears were falling off. During this time, Ahlam and I were seeing less and less of one another. She was still going to school and working part-time. In a way, I was glad and in a way, I wasn't. It isn't easy to find a good woman.

One weekend after I got off work, I went to the park on Manchester and Western Avenues to play basketball. After playing a few games, I was approached by a young girl asking me my name. After looking at her, I said, "I am old enough to be your daddy and why are you asking?"

"My cousin wants to meet you not me."

"Where is she?"

"Over there."

"Is your cousin deaf?"

"No."

"Why didn't she come and ask me herself?"

"I guess she was too scared."

"What's your name?"

"Amelia."

"Well, Amelia, you have more heart than your cousin does," I said, and walked over to meet her cousin.

Her name was Linda. We talked for a few hours and exchanged phone numbers. A week later, we hooked up and went to the movies and dinner and then we took a walk on the beach. About 11:30 p.m., we called it a night. After getting back to her place, she asked if I wanted to come in for a while.

"Next time. It's been a long day and if I come in, I might not want to go home." I gave her a kiss. She smiled at me and went inside. After I got home, I could not stop thinking about her. She had two kids and she was taking care of her cousin. "I can live with that," I said to myself. About eight months later, she and I were as one. I was thankful that I had my job with Brother Mohammed.

* * *

We moved in together after finding a place on 114th and Normandie Avenue. It wasn't much, but it was a start. Samantha, her daughter, was four years old and her son, Jonathan, was eight and Amelia was fifteen years old. We became one big happy family. As time moved on, I noticed that Linda's stomach was getting bigger and bigger. After doctor's visit, I leanred she was seven months pregnant. On January 4,1999 a seven-pounds, six-ounce baby girl was born. I was right there by her side to see Tasha come out of her womb. After the nurse cleaned up Tasha, she handed her to me. I cried like a baby. She was so precious; I didn't care if she wasn't mine. My heart was already stolen.

It wasn't going to be easy having to go to work every day and take care of the house and kids until Linda was able, but I was happy that Tasha was a part of the family now. After getting home from the hospital and getting Linda into bed, I cooked for the kids and spent the rest of the day looking after Tasha. As time moved on, Tasha's real father came around a few times, but we all knew that he did not want the responsibility of a child. After about six months, he stopped coming to the house. It did not matter in Tasha's eyes, as she already knew I was going to be "daddy." As time moved on the kids were getting larger, the apartment was getting smaller and it was time to move. We found another place off Vermont Aveue and Century Boulevard. The only thing I didn't like was that there was only one bathroom.

Three months later, Linda and I were in the kitchen playing a card game called speed. From the corner of my eye, I saw a shadow running under the couch. It was so fast I thought I was seeing things, so I disregarded it. Then I saw it again and I asked Linda if she had seen it.

"What?"

"Something ran underneath the couch," I said, and before I could get the words out of my mouth, we saw a rat run under the couch. Cards went flying all over the kitchen floor.

Linda jumped on top of the kitchen table, yelling, "It's a rat! It's a rat! oh my, God! D, you have to get that thing out of here!"

Well come to find out that was the third rat that had ran under the couch.

As I was walking to the bedroom to check on the kids, another rat ran right past me. Shit it made me jump and it had come from the kids' room. After I turned on the light and woke the kids up, I saw another one jump from the window to the floor. I told Amelia to get the kids up. I saw another one jump from the window to the floor. I told Amelia to get the kids out of here because rats were jumping in through the window. Why did I say that? Amelia jumped out of bed screaming. She took off running to the kitchen without Samantha, Tasha or Jonathan. Damn! I told Jonathan to get up. He was asleep on the top bunk, and he didn't move. I made him get up and took him into the kitchen with his mom and sisters. I went back into the kids' room and pulled back the curtains. There were at least twenty rats stuck between the window and the screen. Seeing all of those rats scared the hell out of me.

I pushed the window closed and called for Linda so she could come and see what I was seeing. It was like watching the movie *Ben*, seeing all of those rats.

She said, "No thanks!"

Over nine rats had made it into the house. I kept count from the first three that had ran under the couch. We didn't have any mouse traps so I had to go to the store. Everybody was stationary on the kitchen table. I told them to keep their eyes open so they could tell me where the rodents had run to. The store was not far, so it only took me twenty minutes to get back.

After I got inside the house, I put sticky traps everywhere. I grabbed the broom and started hitting everything in sight. The stove, the refrigerator, I was trying to get them to come out and run onto the sticky traps. It took me two hours to catch eight rats.

I was exhausted and I thought I was going to go deaf from the volume of the banging noise, and their asses were still on the kitchen table, talking about its some more somewhere. I just gave them my "shut the hell up" look. I looked everywhere for the last rat and the apartment looked like a tornado had hit it. I said to myself, "Maybe I over counted," so I told them that it was safe to get down and walk around. I started cleaning the kids' room first.

Just as I pulled back the cover of Jonathan's bed, a rat jumped down onto the floor, and the screaming ensued.

This time they ran into the bathroom and the rat made his way to the kitchen and ran right behind the stove onto the sticky trap. Man was I happy. I tried to show them that I had caught the last one, but they wouldn't open the bathroom door. After washing up, everyone went back to bed.

"Did you all think that I was going to clean this up after playing exterminator man?"

Nobody answered me, so I went to bed, too.

Four months later, Linda and I started arguing all the time and like always it was over something stupid. I started going to the casino so I wouldn't have to hear her mouth.

A month later, a son of one of her friend's moved in with us. That was another mouth to feed, with no extra income. Things got worse between Linda and me. We broke up after being together for only one and half years, but I assured her that the kids would always be a part of my life. It did not matter to me whether we were together or not, Tasha was already calling me daddy.

Some nights I was the only one who could get her to sleep. If she weren't beside me, she would just cry. The kids were not happy and Linda's family was upset about us breaking up. I told them the same thing that I had told Linda, so they were happy to hear that we went our separate ways.

After about a year of working with Muslims, I had gained a lot of knowledge regarding how they greet, how they prayed four to five times a day, and also their language and activities. I learned a lot about the types of books they read, the clothes they wear and the foods they eat and why. Everyone who knew me was telling me that I was ready to become a Muslim, but something inside me was telling me I didn't have to do that. It was hard for me to explain to some people about this feeling I had in me. Sometimes I didn't even feel like myself; like someone else was inside of my body and I still didn't see a clear picture of why I was there.

A few days later while I was at work I got a call from Mom telling me that she had cancer. I had been gone for three years. Mom told me not to worry that everything was going to be all right. My eyes filled with tears as I listened to her voice. I told Mom I was catching the next flight out to Atlanta, Georgia, but she told me no. She was going to the Cancer Center in Dallas, Texas. I told her to call me when she got there. She said okay and told me that she loved me.

A few days went by and I still hadn't heard from Mom, so I called her and there was no answer. After a week I got a call from Mom's husband telling me that Mom had passed away. They never made it to Dallas. I dropped the phone on the floor. I couldn't believe I would never see her alive again.

After I got myself together, I picked the phone up off the floor. Her husband was telling me that he was going to arrange for me to take a plane to attend Mom's funeral. It would be in one week. I said okay and hung up the phone.

I told Brother Mohammed that my mom had passed away and I had to leave in about a week.

"I'm sorry to hear that, Brother D."

One week later, I was on a plane headed to Atlanta. When I arrived in Atlanta my mother's sister, Aunt Gloria, picked me up from the airport. I hadn't seen her in about five years. It felt good to see her again. After getting to the house and seeing all the family, I felt like I was home again.

A few days after Mom's funeral it was time for me to fly back to Los Angeles, but I didn't have enough money to catch a plane. Instead, I took the Greyhound bus. In a way, I'm glad that I had to take the bus back home. It gave me a chance to think and time to clear my head. I thought of all of the places I had been. I remembered my first time going on a trip alone by bus. It was 1987. I was in my early twenties. Mom and her high school sweetheart had reunited and gotten married.

I never thought a man would take Mom away from me. She told me that they were going to move. She did not say "we" were moving so I knew that it was time for me to wake up and smell the coffee. They went their way and I went mine. I went to visit my grandmother. She had moved to Stanford, Florida. I stayed there for about one year before going back to the east coast to Virginia to stay with my cousins.

About six months later, I was back on the bus. This time I was headed down south to Houston, Texas. I didn't have any family or friends that I could stay with, but that was where I wanted to go. I had no fear of going to different cities or states. I just loved to travel. I guess it ran in my family. As a child, Mom and I would move somewhere new almost every year.

It took me about a week to find a job in Houston. I found one working as a security guard. I moved from the motel room I was staying in and found a room for rent.

After a year, I got tired of being in Houston so I moved to Chicago. Being in Chicago was like being in New York. Everybody was trying to get their hustle on. After only two weeks of being in Chicago, I jumped back on the Greyhound. Usually, I'd call Mom and let her know exactly where I was but from the first day, I knew I would not be in Chicago too long. There was too much going on there for me. I was trying to decide where I was headed then I thought about beaches and women in bikinis. I decided to go to Miami. Yeah, that was the place for me.

After I got to Miami, I called Mom, and she yelled out "Miami? I thought you were in Houston." I told her I had been gone from there for almost a month that I'd stopped in Chicago but didn't like it and came to Miami. Mom said, "Boy, where did you get all of that gypsy blood from?" I started laughing. After I talked to Mom, I walked around looking for a cheap motel. After I found one, I took off for the beach. It was like being in paradise. I walked up and down the beach until the sun went down.

A few days later, I found some temporary work doing construction. Every day after work, I would head to the beach. I stayed in Miami for almost a year. Then I was back on the bus. Tampa, Florida here I come. After seven months of being in Tampa, I headed back to Washington, DC. When I got there, I called Mom and asked her for my aunt's phone number. She told me that my aunt had moved to Maryland. After we hung up, I called my aunt and she told me how to get to her house. After getting to my aunt's house and seeing everybody, it felt pretty good to be with my family again. A week later, I found a job. I knew I wasn't going to stay very long. I didn't want to wear out my welcome. After a few months had I told my aunt I was moving on. She asked me where I planned on going and I told her Dallas, Texas.

"Boy, I'll be glad when you find yourself and settle down somewhere. You know that's where all of the family is, so let me give you the phone numbers I have for them."

When I got to Dallas, I settled down. I stayed for six years. Mom came down a few times and by then my Grandmother had moved to Dallas. My aunt moved from San Antonio, Texas. Everybody was moving back south except Mom and her husband. After six years, I went to Atlanta, Georgia to see Mom and that was the final stop because from that time on I just didn't travel around the world anymore. I followed a vision that led me to

Los Angeles, California. I would have to say that we are all put somewhere for a reason; it's been sixteen years and I'm counting. While riding on the bus thinking back on all my travels, the bus finally arrived in Los Angeles.

I was exhausted when I got home, so I took a shower and went to bed. I woke up the next morning about 9:30 a.m. and got ready for work. When I got to the restaurant, Brother Mohammed wasn't there. He still hadn't made it by 11:00 a.m., so I gave him a call. He informed me that he was no longer open for business.

"Damn, are you serious? What am I supposed to do? My rent is due next week."

"Brother D, I'm sorry."

After I hung up the phone, I said, "When it rains it pours."

I had to move out of my place because I couldn't afford to pay the rent. I was right back where I started. I was so upset I started cursing God and asking what He wanted me to do. "Why did you choose me?" I yelled into the sky so much that day that I lost my voice. I cried myself to sleep. No one knows what tomorrow will bring. That's why we have to live day by day.

After a few days of sleeping in my car, I found a room for rent, but I had to find a job fast. I still was not myself. I was still very upset over losing Mom and everything else. I knew if I didn't keep a clear head I would not be able to move forward in my life. After about a week of looking in newspapers and going to the EDD office, I said to myself, "I don't need a job." I knew how to make money on the side. All I need is a carpet cleaner, a vacuum, a spot remover and a shampooer. After finding a store that sold those supplies, the one I wanted was more than what I had in my pocket. I needed $250.00 more, so I put down what I had on it and told him I'd be back in a week.

The next day an old friend of mine called me and asked if I was free for the weekend. She needed help catering a party up in the hills. The following weekend, working in Beverly Hills was my first time being around people with million dollar homes. After meeting Mr. Vaughn and looking around the house, I could not believe my eyes. People were arriving so I had to get to work. After working Friday and Saturday, Mr. Vaughn asked me if I would like to work a few days out of the week for him driving him around in his limousine. I accepted and he gave me a check for the weekend. It was supposed to be $200.00 but it was for $300.00.

"Thank you! This is what I needed t to get my carpet-cleaning machine."

"Oh you clean carpets?"

"Yes."

"Good now you have another job."

As I was walking to my car I gave Carla a big hug and a kiss.

"What's that for?"

"Thanks to you I can get my carpet-cleaning machine and Mr. Vaughn hired me to be his limo driver a few days out of the week."

"I already know. He asked me a lot of questions about you so I already knew he liked the way you worked."

"Well thank you again."

I headed home with a big smile on my face. The following day I went to pick up my machine then I had some flyers made. I drove all over Los Angeles putting flyers on cars, buildings, anywhere I could find. By the end of the day, I got a phone call asking if I could clean three rooms the following day. Only God knew what was in store for me next.

Chapter 5

———◆◆◆———

Life of the L.A. Gangs and
Innocent Kids Killed by Drive-bys

After a few months of cleaning carpets and working for Mr. Vaughn, I started getting phone calls on a daily basis. Most of the people who called were from bad neighborhoods. One of my first was on 110th and L Street. Everywhere you looked all you saw was graffiti of gang signs and groups of youngsters talking street talk. As I was walking to the building, all eyes were on me so I had to break the ice.

"What's up? Anybody know where Jeannie stays?"

One of the youngsters said, "That's Mom, you the carpet cleaner?"

"Yeah. Brother D…that's me."

As I was walking into the apartment with her son all I heard were gunshots then a car's tires peeling off. People were running everywhere and screaming "L.T. got shot!" After things calmed down a little and everybody was walking to the front of the building waiting for the police and ambulance to come I walked to the front. The boy who'd gotten shot was lying on the sidewalk with a towel wrapped around his leg. I said, 'Thank God he is still alive." Then people started walking across the street where a Hispanic male was lying on the ground. He wasn't as lucky as L.T.

After the police got there Jeannie told me to come back another time. "They are going to tape off the block. You'd better leave before they do it or you will be stuck here all night."

"Okay just call me when you are ready."

After getting home I sat in the car thinking about what happened today. It was like watching a movie, seeing that boy hurt and that Hispanic man dead was too much to bear.

The following weekend I went to work up in the hills for Mr. Vaughn. This guy threw more parties than Hugh Hefner. The life these high class people lived was like a DJ Quick song. The weekend comes and they're doing the same old thing again. A lot of people would look at this as the good life. Living in mansions, millions of dollars under your belt, partying like a rock star three to four times a week and having almost everything you want in life. But I noticed that Mr. Vaughn wasn't happy and it showed in his eyes (the eyes don't lie). I said to myself, "This man has everything you could dream of so what's missing in his life?"

After the party Mr. Vaughn gave me my check.

"Thank you." I paused. "Can I ask you a question? Have you ever been in love?"

Mr. Vaughn looked at me. "Why did you ask me that?"

"You seem to be a man who has everything, but I can see in your eyes that something is missing in your life."

"You are right," he said, and then walked off.

I had completed the job I'd come to do so I left.

The following week I was doing a carpet-cleaning job on Crenshaw and 26th Street. As I was putting my equipment into the truck and saying "So long" to the kids that lived in the house I had just cleaned, five gunshots rang out and the kids ran into the house. I ducked down by my truck. Then I looked down the street. I said to myself, "Damn, not another kid."

People started walking down the street and so did I. First I saw a skateboard in the middle of the street, then I heard a lady scream "No, no, no not my baby!" As I looked to my left there was a little boy lying in the street—dead. I found out he was fourteen years old. I got in my truck and went for a long ride. While I was driving, a song came on the radio by 2Pac Shakur. Staring at the world through my rear view mirror while I was listening to the song, different words started coming out of my mouth. It's called free styling. I pulled over to the side of the road, trying to write down what I was saying.

After the song went off, I said to myself, "I have that song." After finding it, I played that song over and over again. By the time I made it home, I had a song of my own. This was no rap song. This was a message to the streets of Los Angeles. I named the track "L.A. Tear Drops." The following day, I checked around at a few studios. The prices were much too high for my pocket. While driving around, I found another studio. This guy was talking my language. I told Ray, the owner and the engineer of the studio, to give me a week, as I had to get the kids together.

"Okay cool, call me when you're ready," he said.

This had made my day.

After getting home, I walked down the block looking for a few kids I knew. After finding two of them, I told them, "I needed four more kids plus you come to my house after you find four more." After the kids made it to the house, we practiced the song for two hours. I told them that after school I would be by each one of their houses to meet their mom or dad so they would know me and know what was going on.

After five days of practicing the song, the kids were ready. To them and to me this was a dream come true. They were so excited about going into a real studio and being on a track, a few of the parents went with us.

After recording the track, Ray said, "I like that song. Try to get the radio station to play that."

"I'm going to do my best. The next day, a few of the parents called me saying, "D, I had to take that CD from my child. He played it from the time we got into the car until 11:00 last night." I started laughing.

I went back to the studio and asked if I could get two hundred copies made and how much it would cost. Ray told me if I got some blank CDs he would do it for fifty cents a CD.

After burning the CDs, I drove all over L.A. passing them out to schools, churches, at bus stops, everywhere I could think of. I had even put my name on some of the CDs, hoping that someone might call. As days turned into weeks and weeks turned into months not one phone call did I receive. Most of the kids that helped make the CD, listened to it all the time, but no one called me about wanting to buy one. I didn't let it get me down. I just said, "It's not my time yet."

One day after I got home from work a young man walked up to my truck looking for work. His name was Bobby. He was twenty-two years old.

"Brother D, do you have some extra work I could help you with?"

"Give me a phone number where I can reach you and I will call you and let you know." ThenI asked him, "What do you know how to do?"

"Paint, clean a little and drywall."

A few days later, I got a phone call about doing a cleaning job. It was a five-bedroom house. So I called Bobby. I didn't know Bobby that well. I saw him walking in the neighborhood from time to time. On our way to the house to do the job, Bobby and I had a man-to-man talk. I found out that he used to be in a gang, but he had gotten out of it. He was trying to do the right thing now. I asked him if he ever killed anyone and he said no. From that day on, I took Bobby under my wing. We did a few jobs together. Bobby was a good worker and he was a good person, too.

One night about 9:30, I got a phone call from a lady named Ms. Alley who had gotten my number off the flyers I distributed. Her living room had flooded and she wanted to know if I could take care of the problem. I agreed to go so after getting her address I began loading my truck and drove to Compton. I found Ms. Alley's street and began looking for her address. While doing that I noticed a pair of sneakers hanging from the wires of a telephone pole. There was graffiti at almost every stop sign I saw.

I had no idea what gang ruled this territory; it really didn't matter. When you've been on the streets as long as I have, it's all the same. I was having a problem finding Ms. Alley's house, so I called her from my cell phone. She told me I had gone too far and to turn around and drive back the other way and she would be standing where I could see her. I told her I was in a white pick-up truck so she would be able to identify me if I didn't see her first. After going back a few blocks, there she was flagging me down. After I parked and got out of my truck, she apologized to me. She said she'd forgotten that someone had removed the address numbers off her building.

After we were inside her apartment, I asked what had happened. She said her kids were playing in the living room with a baseball bat and it hit the sixty-gallon fish tank, broke the glass and water went everywhere. I said thank God you live on the first floor and Ms. Alley said thank God, too. On my way to the truck to get the wet vac, I heard three gunshots. I ducked down by my truck. Bullets have no name and only God knows where they are going to land. After not hearing any more shots, I grabbed the wet vac, locked my truck and made my way back to the apartment.

"Did you hear that?"

"Yeah," Ms. Alley said, "that happens all of the time, day and night." I couldn't believe it. Then she told me over ten people were killed in the city of Compton last year and the amount this year is more than that. When you think about it most neighborhoods have two or three different gangs just blocks from one another. I know it sounds crazy, being this close to one another. Why not join forces for the good of the community? There would be less crime in the neighborhood; you would be able to walk down the next block without looking over your shoulder.

We should be looking out for each other instead of hurting one another. The children would be able to play safely with each other and members of the neighborhood could protect one another. As it stands now the kids are on lockdown because of the conflicts between the different gangs on different blocks. Joining forces makes sense to me but what makes sense and what is actually going on are two different things.

It took me about two hours to vacuum the floor dry.

"Where are your kids?"

"On lockdown."

"Funny you should say that."

"What do you mean by that?"

"When you think about it, they are still on lockdown when they play outside because of the gangs."

"I never looked at it like that. But you're right, my kids don't leave off the block we live on and when the sun goes down they know they better be in the house."

"Well we must keep on doing one thing and that is to pray."

I handed Ms. Alley my card, and told her to call me if she needed me.

After getting home, once again, my brain would not shut down. I was trying to come up with ideas to bring different gangs that lived in the same neighborhood together as one. I just knew in my heart there had to be a way to turn all of that negativity into something positive. All the stuff that was going on simply made no sense at all. It seemed to me that almost everyone involved was crying for attention in some form or fashion. No matter what, some of them were willing to do almost anything under the sun to be noticed no matter how senseless the act was. I couldn't stay awake all night so finally I fell asleep.

A few days later, I received a call from someone who wanted carpet cleaning. It was a lady by the name of Ms. Lauren. She lived in Inglewood off England Street. Once I began cleaning her carpet, she asked me if I had any kids. I told her yes all girls.

"Oh my God, I have all girls, too. How many do you have?"

"You can say I have three."

"Wow! I have three girls, too."

We talked about kids in today's world. She told me about what she'd gone through with her three girls.

"My oldest daughter, Jaime, fifteen, went to a party with her boyfriend"

"Wait, did you say fifteen?"

"Yes, fifteen, now can I finish my story?"

I turned off the carpet cleaner and she told me to have a seat.

"Like I said, my daughter went to a party with her boyfriend. He was a member of a gang and she told me that they were standing in the front yard and decided to sit in his car. My daughter, her boyfriend and two other friends, and before you know it another car pulled up beside them and started shooting at them. My daughter was shot in the back four times and one of the bullets could not be removed or she might have become paralyzed or possibly died.

"I live with this every day, wondering if she would make it through from day to day. But that is just the beginning. My second daughter, Sophia, started hanging out with gangbangers when she was only nine years old. She got arrested for going over this girl's house and dragging her out of the door after her mother answered. Then she started beating her. My daughter blackened the little girl's eye and when the girl's mother tried to break up the fight, my daughter started beating on her. The girl's mom ran in the house and called the police. My daughter was still beating on her daughter when the police arrived. Sophia was taken to jail and I got a call from the police station."

"I could not believe what I was being told. I said, my child is only nine years old are we talking about the same girl? When I went to get Sophia, I talked to the other girl's mother and I was at a loss for words. From that day on, my child was uncontrollable. She wouldn't listen to a word I said. I didn't know what to do. Every friend she had was in a gang. All of this time, I had been thinking that my child was going to school every morning. Boy you think you know your kids and sometimes that just isn't so.

"When my daughter Jennifer was thirteen years old, I was in the kitchen cooking dinner while she and her gangbanging boyfriend were visiting on the porch. The next thing I knew she was standing behind me with a knife pointed at my back. She told me not to move or she would kill me. I said, 'Jennifer, what are you doing?' She said, 'Shut up, before I stab you.' I was standing there in tears. I could not believe my own daughter had turned on me. After I started crying, she took the knife away from my back and walked outside. I ran to my room, slammed the door, started crying and asking God what I'd done to deserve that.

Later that night, Jennifer came in my room and said, 'Momma, my boyfriend told me to do that. He said I have to be tough if I want to belong to the gang.' I didn't say anything to her. I didn't know what to say. I went through hell with my kids—all three of them dropped out of school. I'm so glad they are out of my life. I love them, but I don't want to see any of them until the day I die."

* * *

After a year of working for Mr. Vaughn and doing my carpet cleaning on the side, Bobby found a job working in a senior building. I was so happy for him. I also found another job, but would have to move to Riverside to take it. It was a full-time position with free rent. I felt like it was time for a change. In the past year, I had seen more yellow tape, pictures and candles on the street than I could count. I went to work for Mr. Vaughn up in the hills one last time. He told me to keep in touch.

A week later, I moved to Riverside. After moving into my place and checking out the neighborhood, I went for a ride to see which stores were close by. Everything was just a few blocks away. The mall, the grocery store, the park and the gym were all so close to where I now lived it blew me away. After getting back to my new place, people in the complex asked me if I was the new maintenance man.

"Yes, I'm Brother D, and you are?"

"I'm Ms. Evans; they call me OG Grandma."

I laughed. "Why?"

"I don't take no shit from anyone."

"Oh, okay that's good to know."

"I hope you're better than the last one we had."

"Well, I will do my best."

After Ms. Evans walked away, I started thinking one hundred thirty-five units…this will be a lot of work, twenty-four-seven. But I know that I can handle it.

After a few weeks of working on my new job, the tenants became familiar with me and I became familiar with them. I knew who was good, who was bad and who was ugly. Like always, kids started following me around looking for something to do. So I would have them pick up all the trash around the building and then water the grass. Kids get bored fast, so to keep them out of trouble I kept them busy. I'd give them a few bucks for the ice cream truck and on Fridays, I would get them a pizza.

Before you know it, it went from three kids to nine kids wanting to clean the grounds. I said to myself, "What have I started?" As time moved on I began doing work on the side in another building where I met three ladies that became a part of my life—Tracey, Verna and Francis. As I was painting an empty unit, Verna walked in.

"Hi, are you the new maintenance man?"

"No, I'm just doing some side work for the owner. Can I help you with something?"

"Please don't talk about that bitch."

My eyes got big.

"She's telling me that I have to move because she doesn't like my boyfriend."

"What happened?"

"Someone told her that my man be beating my ass like I'm a dog."

"Well, is it true?"

"No! That bitch is just jealous because I have a man and she doesn't. She stands by my window at night trying to hear if we're having sex. Tracey told me just the other day that she saw her standing by my window when she took out her trash. She started walking fast back to her apartment when she saw Tracey."

"Damn, are you serious?"

"Yes I am. Can you help me find a place?"

"We have some empty units. How many bedrooms do you need?"

"Two. One for me and one for my daughter."

I told her that I would bring her an application, and she thanked me.

The next day during my lunch break, I took Verna an application and told her I would pick her up when she was ready. When I got back to work, the kids were getting off the school bus. Considering the time, I guess they only went for half a day. They were all headed my way. All I heard was, "Brother D! Brother D, can we help you do something?" It was just so many of them, so I gave them all a trash bag and told them I would buy two pizzas when I got off, but no more than two.

After getting off work and getting pizza for the kids, Verna called saying she was done with the application. I got to Verna's and while I was looking over the application, her daughter walked into the kitchen where we were sitting.

"Hi, Brother D."

As I turned around to see who was speaking to me, my heart started beating like a drum. When I saw Verna's daughter Francis, my heart nearly dropped. She looked just like Mae, my goddaughter who passed away a few years earlier. Francis was born with Scoliosis.

"I told her your name."

I could not take my eyes off Francis. All I saw was Mae.

"Are you okay," Verna asked me.

I told her about Mae, the child who changed my life around.

"Oh, D, I'm sorry to hear that."

I told Verna I would give her application to the manager in the morning. "All I want for you to do is start packing."

"Okay, thank you."

After getting home, I pulled out Mae's picture and stared at it for a few minutes. My heart went into my throat. My feelings got the best of me. Only God knew what that child meant to me. A week later, Verna and Francis moved into the building. I asked Verna if she needed any help and she told me that her boyfriend was taking care of everything. I stayed over Verna's place for a few hours talking to Francis.

I told Francis about all the kids in the complex and promised her that the next time we went to the park she could come with us. Francis started clapping. I told her that I had to go home, but I would see her tomorrow.

"You promise?" Francis said.

"Yes, I promise."

A month later, Francis was now a part of my life. One thing that puzzled me was Verna's boyfriend. I had not seen him yet, so I asked Verna about her boyfriend.

"He is in Phoenix taking care of his father until they could find someone to take over."

"That's good to know. That tells me that he's an okay guy."

"When he wants to be."

"Oh okay. I'm going to leave that one alone."

One week later as I was cleaning the grounds, Verna's boyfriend showed up. Francis was standing in her bedroom window waiting for me to pass by. She always knew when it was time for me to collect the trash from her side of the building and she'd be there to say, "Hi, Brother D." I would always ask her what was going on. But this morning after Francis greeted me, I heard a man's voice saying, "Get your ass out of that window! Who are you talking to?"

"It's Brother D," Francis said, and then I heard Verna say, "She always stands in the window in the morning waiting on

Brother D to pass by. He's the one that got me in here. I told you he's like family." I didn't hear anymore after that so I just walked away. I was saying to myself, "Whoever he is, he doesn't sound like a good person to have around Francis."

As time moved on I was not seeing Francis in the window anymore in the mornings. I had also stopped seeing Verna. So after I got off work I went over to Verna's place. After knocking on the door, Verna's boyfriend opened it. His name was Tommy.

"What's up, Brother D? I'm Verna's boyfriend Tommy."

"Cool is Verna home?"

He called her to the door. Francis ran to the door when she heard my name.

"Brother D! Brother D," said Francis.

"Hi, Francis." While Francis was giving me a hug I could see out the corner of my eye that Tommy didn't like what he was seeing.

Finally, Verna came to the door.

"Hi, stranger. I have not seen you outside in a while. What's going on?"

Verna said, "I was going to call you. I need to go to the grocery store. Can you take me?"

"Sure. Let me go and get my truck. I'll meet you in the parking lot in five minutes."

After picking up Verna, I asked her where Francis was.

"That's what I want to talk to you about. I don't need to go to the store but it was the only way I could talk to you. Tommy is very jealous of you. You're all that Francis talks about, so Tommy stopped her from standing in the window looking for you. He yells at her telling her that he is her daddy not Brother D and every time the phone rings he thinks that it's you, so he comes and sits next to me while I'm on the phone. Just to see who I'm talking to."

I didn't know what to say. My heart was already breaking into pieces.

"Why are you saying anything?"

"What do you want me to say? That's your man."

After taking Verna to the store and dropping her off at home, I went for a ride to clear my head. I started thinking that maybe Tommy was right. Francis was not my child and the love she shows me is the love he wants her to show him. Maybe I'm taking it away from him. I just have to let go, but I must say that I am going to miss seeing that big smile that Francis has.

A few days later while I was at work, my cell phone rang. It was Verna. I was happy to hear her voice.

"What's up, Verna?"

"Do y'all have another two bedroom apartment for rent?"

"Yes, who's looking for a place?"

"A friend of mine."

"Is your friend there now?"

"Take her to the office to get an application."

"Okay."

One week later, Tracey, her daughter, her grandkids and her man moved in. Verna introduced me to Tracey. She was okay, a little ghetto though. She asked me if I had a cigarette before she even said hi. I said, "Damn, hello to you, too, Ms. Tracey." We all started laughing. As time moved on you would think that Verna and Tracey were both my wives. Tracey was always knocking on my door every day asking for a cigarette or wanting to know what I was cooking. She always wanted to borrow something and Verna always needed to go somewhere—to the store, the bank or wanting to know if Tracey was at my house. These two women were driving me crazy.

"Tracey, doesn't your man get on your ass about you coming over to my place all of the time?"

"No."

"What kind of man do you have?"

"He's in jail. A jailbird man is the kind of man I have." Tracey took a seat on the couch, changed the channel on my television and asked for a cigarette.

"I was watching that. Don't you have a TV at home and don't you have to put your grandkids to bed?"

"No, my daughter is there and my cable is off. What do you have to drink?"

"You know what? I give up, you win. I'll give you a key."

"For real?"

"Hell no," I said and walked into my bedroom to watch television. "Lock the door when you leave."

Four months later at 7:35 a.m., I was cleaning the grounds. I walked around Verna's apartment hoping to see Francis standing in the window. Instead, I heard Verna's man cursing then I heard Verna screaming, then a big boom on the wall. People started coming out of their apartments asking what was going on. Verna screamed again saying, "Don't hit me anymore!" As I was running to Verna's front door, I heard one of the neighbors say, "I'm calling the police." After knocking on Verna's front door and asking if she and Francis were okay she said they were.

"Is Tommy hitting on you?"

"No, I fell."

"Verna, everybody heard you screaming. Why are you lying to me? Where is Tommy?"

"He's in the bedroom."

Before I could say another word, the police were walking through Verna's front door. They asked Verna what was going on and she told the police the same thing she'd told me, which was a lie. One of the officers started asking the neighbors what happened then they asked Verna to tell Tommy to step outside.

The police put Tommy in the patrol car. I guess they were running a make on him. They let him go and he went back inside the house with Verna. The police took off and everybody went back inside their units. As I was walking back to my tool room, Tracey came running, asking me what was going on with Verna. I told Tracey what happened.

"D, don't tell Verna I told you this, but this is the same reason Verna had to move from her last place. Tommy was beating her ass so the manager kicked him off the property."

"So why would Verna let him back in her life?"

"That's why I don't go over her house. I can't stand that motherfucker. You got a cigarette, D?"

"Here Tracey, take the whole pack I've got another one."

After I got off work, I called Verna. There was no answer. I tried again an hour later and this time I got a busy signal. I know Verna or Tommy took the phone off the hook. So I just took my mind off it. The following weekend I hadn't seen Verna all week so I called Tracey. I told Tracey to meet me by the tool room and before she could ask, I said, "Yes, I have a cigarette. Just get your ass over here!"

After Tracey made it to the tool room, I said, "Look, this is what I want you to do. You owe me so I don't want to hear no out of you."

"What is it that you want for me to do?"

"Go knock on Verna's door and here take this cup with you and ask if you can borrow some sugar."

"Damn, D, are you a psychic? How did you know that I needed some sugar?"

"Just go and see if Verna is okay."

As Tracey walked to Verna's house I just chilled out in the tool room and waited for her to get back.

An hour later Tracey returned to the tool room.

"How are Verna and Francis?"

"They're fine. Tommy was gone so Verna and I got a chance to talk. She told me to tell you that she will call you and Francis said, 'Hi.'"

"Okay, that's good to hear. Now I can relax my brain." I dug inside my pocket. "Here, Tracey, take this five dollars and go get yourself a pack of cigarettes."

"Thanks, D. Can I get five more dollars so I can buy myself some beer?"

With the look I gave Tracey she knew that wasn't going to happen.

"Damn, D, don't kill me with that look," she said, and walked away.

After getting off work, I had to help a few kids with school projects so my house was the public library for the rest of the day.

While I was helping the kids my cell phone rang, it was Verna. I told the kids that I had to step out for a few minutes. Verna was telling me not to worry.

"Tommy won't put his hands on me anymore."

"How do you know that, Verna?"

"Because I told him I would call the police if it happened again. He's been cooking my dinner and telling me every day that he is sorry for what happened. Ever since the police questioned him, he has been nice to me."

"As long as you and Francis are safe, that's good enough for me. I'll talk to you later I have a house full of kids that need my attention."

A few weeks later at 11:45 p.m., my cell phone rang. I was asleep.

"Hello?" I answered. It was Linda, an old girlfriend of mine. She was talking so fast I could not understand one word that she was saying. "Slow down and tell me what is going on."

"D, I have an emergency. Please come to L.A. as quickly as you can."

After getting the address, I made my way to the freeway. I tried to call Linda again but I got no answer. It was driving me crazy not knowing what the situation was. When I reached my destination, I saw Linda sitting in her car crying.

"What the hell is going on?"

"D, my boyfriend and I just got into a fight."

"About what?"

"Because he won't get a job and doesn't pay any bills. I told him that he would have to find somewhere else to live. So I put him out."

"Okay, then what?"

Linda would not tell me what had happened after that. "D, I need you to keep the girls for me. Please, D, I don't trust anyone else with my babies and they have always thought of you like a stepfather."

I needed a minute to think. This was a big responsibility and would drastically change my life. I asked Linda where she would be staying and she told me she'd be at her girlfriends.

"I have to stay in L.A. I need to find another house to rent and find a way to get my things out of the other house."

"If you don't want to tell me what's really going on that's fine with me. It seems to be really bad so I'll take the girls with me. Tasha, Samantha get in my truck and I will get your things." The girls were still crying.

While Linda was talking to the girls, I was praying to God for more strength and patience. After making it back to my place, I told the girls they'd have to sleep on the couch that night. It was big enough. "Tomorrow I will clean up the other bed room and get some beds for you two." After getting the kids to sleep, I went back to sleep. I didn't have but three and half hours before I had to get up and get ready for work. Once I was ready to leave, the girls were still asleep. Samantha was twelve years old and Tasha was ten years old. They were old enough to look after themselves. It was a good thing that I worked on the premises where I lived.

I was able to check on them periodically. Every hour I went back in the house to make sure that Tasha and Samantha were fine. About 10:00 a.m., I went in the house and the girls were watching television. They were still lying on the couch. I cooked pancakes, eggs and sausage for breakfast. One of the things that Tasha and Samantha knew about me was that I loved to cook. After the girls finished eating, I went back to work.

I had already told my boss about the girls so she had no problem with me going to check on them. After I got off work,

Tasha, Samantha and I went to the mall to get a few things they needed. When we got back to the house, we started cleaning up the second bedroom.

"Tjo's room will be your responsibility. I don't play clothes on the floor and unmade beds. Make your beds as soon as you get up. The same thing goes for the bathroom; keep it clean. You have yours and I have mine."

After eating dinner, I told the girls that the next day I would bring over a few of the kids that I knew. The kids had already asked who Tasha and Samantha were when they saw them walking into my house. I told them that they were my stepdaughters and that they would meet them the next day. After I got off work, I invited a few of the kids over to meet Tasha and Samantha. As I opened the front door, the girls were singing and dancing to videos they were watching on television. When they saw me, they stopped dead in their tracks. Looking at me like they thought they were in trouble.

"These are my kids—Tasha and Samantha. Girls, this is Glen, Kia, Ruth, T.T. and Juanita." I told them to have fun and to clean up what they messed up. I had to go to the store. When I got back from the store, the kids were outside playing by the front door. It was nice to see them running free and enjoying themselves. It made me feel good. Now I didn't have to worry about them being bored. As I was taking the groceries into the house, Tasha and Samantha came running. They wanted to know what was for dinner. The other kids came running, saying, "Yeah, what's for dinner?"

As I looked around, I said, "I don't know half of you kids and I have to feed you?" They all replied, "Yeah!" So I did what was best for all of us and ordered some pizza.

The kids had taken over my front room so I went in my bedroom to watch television. I had to close my door because of the noise they were making, but I was glad that they were having fun. After a few hours, I told the kids that the party was over and for them to act like Michael Jackson and beat it! After the kids went home, I told the girls to hit the tub and go to bed. "We have a long ride in the morning," I said. They wanted to know where we were going. "To L.A. to see your mom and get the paperwork so I can register you in school. School starts next week."

They were pretty excited about seeing their mom and starting a new school. After we arrived in L.A. and picked up the paperwork from Linda, I told them that I had some runs to make.

"That will give you time with your girls and I'll be back at 8:00 p.m."

"Okay, see you later."

I went to see my home girl, Sandra. She was the best friend a person could have. As I pulled up in the driveway, I heard that crazy dog barking. His name was Poppy, but I called him Can't Get Right. You tell him to sit he lies down. You tell him to stay he runs. That dog was loco, but I liked his crazy butt. As I rang the doorbell, the dog in the house started barking. Her name was Noodle. Sandra opened the front door.

"What's up?" I said.

She was surprised to see me. I didn't tell her I was in town. We talked all day until eight o'clock that night. I told Sandra the next time we would go out to eat. I picked up the girls and we drove back home. I was tired and they were tired so we all hit the sack.

The following Monday I took off work to register the girls into school. The school was not far from the house. I told them that for the first two weeks I would drop them off and pick them up. After the first week of school Tasha and Samantha told me I didn't have to drop them off or pick them up. They made more friends and they could walk to and from school with them.

"That's fine, but go straight to school in the mornings and come straight home when school is out. Make sure you don't get into anyone's car!" They agreed.

As the weeks went by, I started to see more and more kids in my house when I got home from work. Every time I walked into the kitchen they would ask what's for dinner.

"Don't you have a mom, a dad or a grandma that has food in the house?"

"Yeah we do," one child said. "But not all of the kids got home cooked meals."

Some of these kids were going through hard times. Top Ramen, frozen burritos and fast food was all some of them were getting to eat every day. I thank God that I took after Mom when it came to the kitchen. I cooked almost every day for the girls, so a lot of nights I fed a lot of the other kids, too.

As time moved on my house became the youth center. Some days you would think that every kid in Riverside was in my house. When I got off work I did what I would always do, high tail it to my bedroom and close the door. Seeing all of these kids almost every day, and seeing how happy they were just made me wish that they were all mine.

I was still looking out for Tracey and Verna. Tracey had stopped coming to the house to ask for cigarettes or what I was cooking for dinner. She would catch me at work or call me. She knew the kids had taken over the house, so all she asked for was a cigarette now and then or maybe a few dollars. I was still looking out for Verna and Francis also. I took Samantha and Tasha over Verna's a few times to play with Francis. Francis really enjoyed playing with the girls.

About a month later, Verna called and asked me if I could come over. I told her to give me a few minutes. After I got to Verna's place the front door was open.

"Come in, D," Verna said.

As I walked in my heart started beating real fast. "What's wrong? where is Francis?"

"She's in the bedroom asleep."

I exhaled. "Are you and Francis okay? Tell me what's wrong."

"Tommy left me."

Thank you, Jesus, I thought. "I know you loved him only God knows why. I really feel it was for the best."

"D, you're right."

"I tell you what, when I get off work tomorrow how would Francis and you feel about taking a ride with me?"

"Okay, sounds good. I've been in this house all week."

"Cool. I'll pick you guys up at 6:30 p.m."

As I was going into the house I heard Tracey yelling my name. "Yeah, Tracey, what is it?

"Here, D." It was a pack of cigarettes.

"Oh my God this must be your last day on Earth."

Tracey laughed. "I'm not that bad."

I laughed. "Yes the hell you are." After a few minutes of joking around, I told Tracey about Verna and Tommy.

Tracey said the same thing I'd said, "Thank you, Jesus." Then she said, "I'm going to walk over to Verna's and see if she tells me. I need some flour anyway." I just shook my head as Tracey walked away.

The next day after I got off work I told Samantha and Tasha that I had to run. "At 7:00p.m., tell your friends that the party is over and lock the door. Call me if anything goes wrong."

Verna, Francis and I took an hour-long ride on the freeway, listening to music. Francis loved to go for long rides. On the way back home, I stopped to get us something to eat. When it came to food, Francis didn't play, that girl could eat. After we finished eating, I took Verna and Francis home. It was about 9:30 p.m.

The girls were already in bed watching television. I told them good night and that I loved them. I reminded them to say their prayers after they turned off the television.

The following weekend the girls' mom showed up to stay for a few days. I was so happy; I danced a jig. The girls said "D, you so crazy." We were all laughing and having a good time and I told Linda that the girls would show her around. "Peace. I'm out of here." All they felt was the wind passing them as I flew out of the front door. After going to visit a few of my friends, I hit the casino. Four hours of playing poker and the slot machines left me without a dime, but I was still happy. I just lost all of my money, why am I so happy? I should have been pissed off, but I wasn't. Oh well I'll just stop at the ATM then go home.

I walked out of that casino feeling like I'd hit the jackpot. I just felt so free. Now I know the way Mom felt when she would send me away for the summer. Those were not tears of sadness those were "thank you Jesus" tears. I'm free! After leaving the casino, I went for a ride before I went home. It was about 11:00 p.m. when I made it home. The girls and their mom were camped out in the living room watching television. I said good night and went into my room.

A year had come and gone. I was at work one day when Linda called me on my cell phone to tell me to get the girls things packed up because she was on her way to pick them up. Linda found a house.

"That's good news to hear. Where in L.A. is the house? I will bring the girls so they can see it."

"The house is not in L.A. it's in Atlanta."

"What?" I said what at the top of my lungs. "Atlanta, what made you get a place in Atlanta?" Linda told me that was where her mom was and she found the house.

I didn't have any more to say about it. I just said okay and hung up. I told my boss what was going on so she gave me the rest of the day off. I drove to the girls' school and pulled them out of class. After getting them home, I told them the news. They were so happy, but when I told them where the house was they were not so happy. This was the saddest day of the year. About an hour later, Linda showed up. The girls were still packing. They were not in a hurry and I wasn't going to rush them.

"Damn, y'all still packing? What's taking so long?"

"We didn't get to say goodbye to our friends. Why do we have to move to Atlanta?"

"Look I'm sorry, but we have to go."

After helping the girls and then walking them out to the car, Tasha started to cry. She hugged me so tight; there was nothing I could say or do to change things so I just kissed her on the cheek. I told them both that I loved them. As they pulled off, the girls were looking through the back window and I was still waving goodbye.

I'd known Tasha since the day she was born and Samantha since she was four years old. I did not understand what was going on in my life. Ever since day one in L.A., my heart kept getting broken into pieces. I went into the house, took a drink and stretched out on the couch. I was awakened by a loud knock on the door. I looked at the clock. It was 3:30 p.m. I had been asleep for three hours. The kids were out of school and they were at my door. I opened the door and they ran in asking where Samantha and Tasha were. I told them the party was over for good. The girls' mom had come to move them to Atlanta. It was so quiet you could have heard a roach crawling. The kids were broken hearted just like I was. The kids were gone. For the first time in a year, my house was quiet. I didn't know what to do as day turned into night. It was too damn quiet.

The next morning, while brushing my teeth, I realized I forgot to wake up the girls. I ran to the girls' room, saying, "Get up," to an empty room. I had forgotten that the girls were gone. I knew it was going to take me a while to get use to an empty house. After six months, the girls were calling me almost every day. Tracey had begun coming over again trying to take over my kitchen and living room. I stopped by Verna's every day to check on her and Francis, but this day was like no other.

The manager, Ms. Doirs, told me that some people were moving into apartment 332.

"You rented that unit?"

"Yes."

"Who?"

"Two sisters and two kids."

As I was walking to the tool room, I saw the two sisters moving in. One of them said, "Hi, are you the maintenance man?"

"Yeah, everybody calls me D or Brother D."

"I'm Mortisha and that's my sister Lexus."

"Welcome to the Crystal Lake Apartments. If you need anything just let me know."

"Okay," she said and walked away.

As I walked into the tool room, I had a funny feeling in my stomach. It was a feeling like trouble was coming. After a few weeks, that feeling I had in my stomach proved right.

Less than a week, after Mortisha and Lexus moved in it became obvious to me that they were two wild ladies. Even though Mortisha had a daughter, she partied all the time and so did Lexus. Their apartment was constantly full of company. People were always coming and going. The smell of marijuana and cigarette smoke was everywhere. A few times the manager had to tell them about the stench from the marijuana smoke. They always promised that it wouldn't happen again, but it always did. I guess they just couldn't help themselves. No matter how many times I tried to impress upon Mortisha how her behavior was probably affecting her daughter's outlook on her as a mother and on life itself she continued to party. I remember one weekend (I think it was on a Saturday) things got so wild at their apartment I decided to take some of the kids from the block out for pizza so that Mortisha's daughter could join us and get away from the madness for at least one evening.

One day after work, a few kids were waiting by my front door.

"What's going on?" I asked them.

"It's that time again, for our school projects," said Ruth.

I just shook my head. Last year it took me about a week to clean my kitchen from that volcano exploding.

"Did you all tell your moms' where you were going to be?"

The kids said, "Yes," but there was a new face in the bunch.

"Wait one minute, who is that?"

Ruth said, "That's Elsie, she just moved on the block a few weeks ago."

"Is your mom Mortisha or Lexus?"

Elsie said, "Mortisha."

"Did you tell your mom that you were coming to my house?"

"No, but she knows that I'm with Ruth."

"That won't work in my book."

Those kids knew that I didn't play that.

Ruth said to Elsie, "Come on, let's go tell your mom where you are going to be."

While they went to ask if it would be okay for Elsie to be at my house, I fixed myself something to eat.

Suddenly, there was a knock at the door. "Damn, did they fly over there?" As I opened the door, it was Tracey.

"What's up, D?"

"What's up, Tracey?"

She started twitching her nose in the air then she walked into the kitchen. "That sure smells good. Make me one." Then she asked if she could use my phone.

As usual, she sat down on the couch and asked for a cigarette. I sure was glad that I had unlimited texting and calling since Tracey was using the phone. She had no idea that the kids were on their way to the house.

Another knock came at the door and when I opened it the kids came charging in.

"Damn, D, I thought your girls were gone," Tracey said.

"They are its school project time."

"I'm out of here. Bye, D."

I started laughing and the kids wanted to know what was so funny. "Nothing, let's get started on the projects." As I was helping the kids, another knock came at the door. I told Glen to see who it was. Glen opened the door. "It's Elsie's mom," he said, and as she walked in.

"Hi, D, you have a nice place."

"Thank you, Mortisha. Have a seat. We're just finishing up for the day."

"I see you have a way with kids."

"Well in my younger days I worked in a youth center and I was a big brother."

Mortisha asked if I had a girlfriend I told her no, but I was seeing someone. The last part was not the truth, but I had no desire to be bothered by Mortisha. Tracey was enough and I wasn't sleeping with her. What I didn't need in my life was some woman who wanted to party every day combined with Tracey. Shit, I'd be dead. After the kids and Mortisha left, I cleaned up and went to bed. Eight months later, Mortisha was still trying to get at me. Thank God, I think with the head I have on my shoulders.

Fast women are not my thing. During this time, Verna was telling me that her girlfriends were bringing some guy over for her to meet. I told her good luck then I went home. About an hour later, my phone rang. It was Verna. I asked her what was up and she asked me if she could come over because something was wrong with her phone.

"I thought your girlfriends and that guy were over."

"They already left, but he's still here."

"The phone doesn't sound broken to me. What's wrong with it? It keeps going off and on whenever someone calls."

"I don't want to interrupt your evening with your new friend. Call me when he's gone."

Fifteen minutes later, Verna called again. Before I could say anything, she said "D, please come over here."

I knocked on the door and Verna let me in. She wrapped her arms around me and said, "D, he raped me."

My heart fell to my feet. While I was trying to stop Verna from crying so I could get the whole story, Francis walked into the living room. I asked Verna if he had touched Francis, but Verna didn't say anything. She wouldn't stop crying.

I asked Francis, "Did that man touch you?"

"No."

"How long ago did he leave? Was he in a car, walking on a bike?"

Verna told me that he was on a bike.

"What race was he?"

"White."

"Verna, are your sure he was White and not Mexican?"

"He was White."

After calling the police, a few people in the neighborhood and I went looking for the guy. We had no luck. I went back to Verna's place and it was a full house. The police had come and gone, but Verna's daughters were still there. They were on the phone with Verna's two girlfriends. The ones that brought him to Verna's house. I must have heard every curse word in the book. They were trying to find out where the rapist lived.

Verna's daughters went over to Verna's girlfriend's houses to talk to them. They asked me to stay with their mom until the police came back. After they took off, I went into the bedroom to check on Verna. She was lying on the bed with her face in the pillow.

"Verna, do you want some water?"

"No. I wish you had come when I called you, D. He told me he would hurt Francis if I didn't do what he told me to."

I was so mad at myself I could not think straight. As I walked out of the room, Francis was standing in the hall. I could not even look at her I felt so bad inside. I went back into the living room and sat on the couch. About an hour and a half later, the police came back. They asked Verna for more information. After the police took off, I told Verna to lock her door. I went home and I tried to go to sleep, but my brain would not turn off. All I kept hearing was Verna saying, "Why didn't you come?" About 2:45 a.m., I fell asleep. After getting up about 10:00 a.m. Saturday morning, I called to check on Verna. I asked her if her daughters had come back to her house. She said no so I asked her if she needed anything. She said no and hung up the phone.

I was feeling really bad. I kept asking myself, "Why didn't I go over there? She was trying to give me a hint that something was wrong, but I didn't realize it. I still felt like it was my fault. As time moved on, I took Verna and Francis under my wing and during this time, Mortisha was trying everything to get me to sleep with her. Everyone was telling me that it wasn't my fault; they were noticing all of the time I was spending with Verna and Francis.

I didn't care what people were thinking or saying about me. I was never going to leave her side, not for anything in the world. After I got home, Tracey came over asking me what was up with Verna and me.

"What do you mean?"

"What does she have that I don't? I look better than her."

"Tracey since when have your feelings for me been so deep? Plus you have a man and it's not what people think it is. What does my life have to do with yours or anyone else's? I don't owe you people anything."

Tracey asked for a cigarette then left for home.

As days turned into nights and nights turned into days, I noticed that the kids were not coming by anymore and people in the neighborhood were not speaking to me. Everybody acted like I owed them something. "Damn!" I yelled. "Everybody wants my hand in marriage." I walked into the house. With all of this bullshit going on, I had to watch my back. I just could not believe what was happening. It was like I was surrounded by Satan's children. I knew he wanted my soul, but that didn't stop me from helping Verna.

She told me that everybody hated on her and I told her not to let them win. "Stay strong. For some reason, everybody is jealous of our friendship. Why I don't know."

The next day while I was at work, Mortisha came to the tool room. "Why don't you want me, D, and what's up with you and Verna?"

"Verna is a close friend of mine, you know that. It's not that I don't want to be with you. Your lifestyle and mine are totally different. You already have a man and you just had another baby six months ago."

"He's just a friend."

"Yeah a friend you sleep with every night."

"I want you, D."

"I'm sorry, but I'm not interested, Mortisha."

Mortisha flashed her titties. "You know you want these," she said, and then she walked out of the tool room.

I just looked up and said, "Thank you, God, for the extra strength you have given me."

A few weeks later I got hurt on the job. I had to go to the hospital. They told me I would have to have surgery on my left shoulder. I could still work, but light duty only.

Damn why me? All that did was made things worse than they already were. After two months of light duty, only a few people were still speaking to me. Mortisha was giving me an evil look every time she saw me. Ms. Evans came to me while I was cleaning the grounds.

"D, I know that all of those things I've heard about you are not true. People are just jealous of your personality. Don't let them get to you."

"All of what things?"

"Things like, you beat up on some old woman and took her money, you sleep with all of the kids' moms, you have tricks off the street come to your house...those things. People are also saying that you let gang members over to your house and smoke weed with them."

I started laughing so hard that tears were coming out of my eyes. Ms. Evans started laughing, too.

"D, everybody around here knows that shit isn't true. Somebody doesn't like you and they are trying to get everyone else around here to hate you. Watch your back, D. If I hear or find out who this person is trust me I will let you know."

"Okay," I said and then Ms. Evans went home.

After work, I didn't turn on my TV or my computer. I was sitting on the couch holding my head in my hands. I asked God, "What am I doing wrong?" I sat there until the sun went down, staring at the walls, hoping that God would give me an answer. I didn't have anything to feel guilty about. I knew I had not done anything wrong. It was like Ms. Evans said, some of the people around here didn't like me and I'd have to watch my back. What I did not understand was if they took a look around they would see in this neighborhood I'm already dead.

The kids don't come by anymore, people who I thought were my friends don't speak or call anymore, except Ms. Evans. Mortisha, my employer and my co-workers also turned on me. So what do I have left that they want? I know that it's not God. They don't have to go through me to reach the Almighty. So I guess I will never know. I only had a few more days left on my job. The next day while I was at work, Verna called and asked me to come by and meet her daughter. I told her I would be there in the meantime. Everyone walked by me like I was an alien.

Some of the kids would wave at me with sad looks on their faces. They knew I wasn't the bad guy in this picture. They had to do what their parents told them to do so I didn't wave back I just looked at them and smiled. After getting to Verna's place, I met her daughter Sherla. She would be staying with Verna for a while. I was happy to hear that. Now I wouldn't have to worry about her when I had my surgery. I told Verna I would be moving.

"You know this is the last week of work and I will no longer be employed here. After this weekend, I won't be able to pay rent for a two-bedroom place. I found another place across town. That is where I will be staying until I heal from my surgery."

Verna gave me a hug and started crying. She told me she was going to miss me and I told her I would miss her, too.

"Where's my buddy Francis?"

"Francis is in her room asleep."

I went to Francis' room and kissed her on the cheek before going back to work.

When I got back to work Mortisha walked up to me. What's going on?"

"When are you working your last day?"

"Why do you ask?"

"I just want to know."

"Friday."

She said, "Okay," and walked away.

After I got off work, I went home and packed. By 11:30 p.m., I was through moving. I was so tired I just crashed on the living room floor. About 5:15 a.m., I woke up from a pain in my back that was caused from sleeping on the floor. I only had one more hour before I had to be up and get ready for work so I just stayed up.

Before going to work, the pain in my back was gone and I was feeling okay. After I clocked in, my boss asked if I had moved.

"Yes, last night."

"Why?"

"After tomorrow I won't be working here anymore and I can't afford to pay the rent for a two-bedroom apartment."

"Okay, just make sure I get the keys."

"You will," I said, then I went to work.

The day had come and gone. Nothing was different. Brother from another, you could say.

After I got home, I was up for half the night just thinking. About 1:30 a.m., I went to sleep. At 6:00 a.m., I woke up to the sound of my alarm clock. I walked out of my door at 6:30. It was 7:00 a.m. when I pulled up into the parking lot by the front office. At 7:`15 a.m., my boss pulled up. After clocking in, I did what I usually do. I cleaned the grounds, but today was a strange day. It was like I was walking through the valley of the shadow of death. It was so quiet. By 10:00 a.m., people were walking around the place just staring at me. Some I knew and some I didn't. About 10:15 a.m., I walked to the office and the front door was locked. Ms. Woods, my boss, was not in the office. For five years this door has never been locked. While standing by the office waiting for Ms. Woods to come back, a guy walked up to me.

"Can you give me a jump?" he asked.

"Where is your car?"

"In the back parking lot."

"I'm shocked you asked me."

"Why?"

"I'm supposed to be the bad guy around here, you know that."

He just looked at me.

"Let me tell my boss then I'll be around there."

About 10:30 a.m., Ms. Woods returned to the office. I told her about the guy needing a jump, and that I'd be in the back lot. When I pulled around to the back, there were six guys standing around the car. Two more were sitting in a car next to the car that needed a jump. I didn't know any of them except the one who asked me for the jump.

I was trying to figure out why he was asking me for help when he had someone right there with him who was in a car. As I pulled up he walked over to my truck and told me he no longer needed a jump. I said okay and pulled off.

About noon, it was like a ghost town around the complex. There were no kids outside playing, nobody was walking around, but the strangest thing about the whole day was that I didn't have any fear. About 12:30, I went to the office. Ms. Woods was on the phone. She told whomever she was talking to that she would call them back later.

"What's going on today? Nobody's outside, none of the kids are playing; you would think it's the last day on Earth."

Ms. Woods looked at me then said, "D, stay in the office until you're ready to go home. You don't have to work all day."

After hearing that I knew what time it was, I just didn't want to believe it. All that I've been through since the first day of coming here to Los Angeles, I couldn't see it ending this way. At 1:30 p.m., I told Ms. Woods I was going home. All she said was okay. Not a goodbye or good luck with your surgery, not even a handshake. As I was walking to my truck, I took one long last look around thinking about all the positive things that happened here in the last five years. That put a smile on my face. I jumped into my truck and drove off.

I had surgery and six months later, I was finished with my physical therapy. I called an old friend of mine named Sandra and told her I was on my way to Los Angeles. She asked if I would have time to pay her a visit and I told her I did. After arriving in Los Angeles, I went to Skid Row with a truckload of clothes. After parking on Fifth Street, I realized that the number of people that were down there had tripled. When I asked if anyone there need clothes, people started running to the truck. Normally I passed out one shirt and one pair of pants to each person, if I had their size, but there were so many people reaching and grabbing I just gave them the bags. As usual, the people were fighting over the clothes, so I just took off. After I left Skid Row, I went to Sandra's house. As soon as I rang the doorbell those dogs of hers started barking up a storm. Neither one of them were bigger than your hand, but they barked like they were six feet tall.

Sandra and I talked about old times for over an hour and then I told her that I would be moving back to Los Angeles soon. My workman's compensation check would be cut in half in a few months. She asked me where I would be staying and I told her I needed to find a room for rent because no one would rent an apartment to someone on a temporary income. Even if they would, I couldn't afford it.

"You can stay here," she said. "I have a room in the back where my son used to stay. All you have to do is clean up."

"How much a month do you want me to pay?"

"You don't have to give me anything."

"I have to give you something."

To show my appreciation, before I left I gave Sandra a hug and a kiss. "Thank you. You are a true friend," I told her.

On my way back home, I said to myself, "Boy God is always on time." After a few months I had to downsize. Everything I had worked hard for had to be sold and what I didn't sale I simply gave away. Once again, I had to start from zero, but I thanked God for the roof I had over my head. I started going to Trinity Baptist Church every Sunday with Sandra. It was a nice church and it brought back a lot of memories from when I was a kid and went to church with Mom. Sometimes I would look at Sandra and picture Mom. No one understood the friendship that Sandra and I had; she was in her seventies and I was in my forties, but we didn't care what anyone thought. When it comes to real friends, there is no age limit.

Eight months went by and I got a phone call from Verna. I hadn't talked to her in a while. The last time I had called her was six months ago and her phone was disconnected. She told me that she had lost her place and her income. I could not believe what I was hearing.

"Where are you living now?" I asked her.

"With my daughter in Los Angeles."

"Where in Los Angeles?"

"On 117th Street."

"That's not far from me. I'm in Los Angeles, too, staying with a friend of mine."

I wrote down her address and made my way to her daughter's house. As I pulled up in my truck, Verna started walking up to the truck and she didn't look too good. She had lost a lot of weight. As I gave her a hug, I said, "When it rains it pours."

"Tell me about it."

"Where is Francis?"

"Staying with family."

It was ironic that the both of us had lost everything, had to start over in life and only lived fifteen minutes apart.

Verna asked me if I had a room for her because her daughter and her daughter's friend were driving her crazy.

"I wish I did. I'm in a little square room. As soon as you open the door the bed is right there. There is no walking room in there, but I'm saving money and next year I can start looking for work."

"Will you come back to see me?

"Why would you say that?"

"I don't know, D, it's just that I'm going through so much right now. I've never been so depressed in my life."

"Verna, look at me. We are in the same boat right now with one paddle and I'm not going to be the only one paddling. I need for you to stay strong and complete this task. Shit I lost everything, too. Do you see me walking with my head down? Do you?"

"No."

"Okay then God put us this close for a reason. I see that now, before I didn't. Together we will be back on top again and when that day comes, we will appreciate our lives even more."

I was so hyped up, Verna's eyes had gotten bigger than her glasses. After I calmed down, I told Verna I would see her in a few days. From that day on, I had taken Verna back under my wing.

As time moved on the New Year was here, it was finally 2012. I hadn't worked for two years and it was time for me to start job hunting before my unemployment benefits ran out. I went to the EDD office and it was packed. I had to wait for over an hour to use the computer. I realized that if I went to the library I could've logged in, so the next day I went to the library and was able to put in applications for six different jobs. By the end of the week, I had applications all over Los Angeles. I figured someone had to call or send me an email within the next week. All week I checked my email, nothing. A week later, I got a phone call from a lady named Ms. Kathy, the owner of a senior citizen complex, asking me to come in for an interview. After my interview, I had a job cleaning property, light duty work, which was just what I needed.

Stopped here After being on the job for one month, it felt like I'd been working there for years. During my lunch break, I played dominoes with the Senior citizens. Sometimes a few people would ask me if I wanted to eat lunch, it was pretty cool working there. One day before I got off work I got a phone call from Ms. Washington. I thought she was calling about a job she'd found me, but then I remembered that she was retired from the EDD. She asked me if I wanted to make some extra money this weekend, and I asked doing what. She said that her cousin, who lived on 76th Street, needed someone to take her Christmas stuff down.

"Are you talking about Ms. Florence?"

"Yes, I forgot that you've been over there before."

"Yeah, I used to put her Christmas stuff up years ago and the lady across the street… what's her name?"

"Pamela is her name."

"It's been so long since I've seen them tell Ms. Florence I will see her on Saturday."

After I got off work, I went to check on Verna. As I pulled up, I saw her sitting on the porch. She saw me before I could finish parking. She asked if I could take her to the store. I told her to get in. I headed for the store and Verna asked me if I would just drive around for a while. We had been on the freeway for at least ten minutes and Verna had not said one word. So I turned up the volume of the music and kept driving. After about an hour and a half the sun was way down.

I had to stop for gas and when we reached the gas station, Verna asked me to buy her a beer and a pack of cigarettes.

"What? When in the hell did you start smoking and drinking?" She started laughing then I started laughing and said, "Shit you had me scared for a minute."

"You should have seen the look on your face. I needed that laugh." She was still laughing.

"Ha, ha, very funny. Just for that catch the bus home."

"Yeah right."

After we got back on the freeway we were stuck in traffic. By the time I dropped Verna off at home, the sun had gone down.

"Thank you for the ride, D. I feel much better."

"Okay, peace."

The following Saturday around noon, I went to Ms. Florence's house and she was happy to see me and I was happy to see her. It had been so long since we'd seen each other. We talked for almost two hours. Ms. Florence loved to talk. I was finally able to start on the Christmas stuff. It took me about two hours to pack everything up and put it away. Then I walked across the street to see Ms. Pamela.

I knocked on the door and someone asked, "Who is it?"

"Brother D. Is Ms. Pamela was home?"

"She is, but she doesn't know you."

"I used to put up her Christmas lights years ago," I said, and then I heard Ms. Pamela's voice saying, "Oh," through the door. "I know who that is, open the door."

The person that opened the door was Ms. Pamela's daughter Ms. Laura. I had never met her before that day. After giving Ms. Pamela a hug, she told me her daughter had moved in with her because she couldn't do the things she used to do anymore. Ms. Pamela was ninety-three years old. We talked for about an hour and a half. I gave her my number and told her to call me if she needed anything.

As time moved on, I was working a full-time job and helping a few friends. I started looking for an apartment close to my job. Everywhere I checked for a single or a one-bedroom, rent was too high. I knew that living in Los Angeles could be expensive. I called a few people I knew, asking if they knew someone that was renting a back house. Ms. Florence told me Ms. Pamela had a two-bedroom in the back of her house that no one was living in. She said it had been empty for a while. I thanked her and made it a point to speak to Ms. Pamela about the back house. After getting to Ms. Pamela's house she started asking me if I could fix this or that. I couldn't get a word in edgewise. The little things she asked me to fix didn't take long. Then I asked her about the house in the back. She told me it needed some work, and told her it wasn't a problem. Then she asked when I planned to move in. I told her as soon as I could. Ms. Pamela said okay.

Two weeks later I moved into my new place. Ms. Florence was so happy that I was right across the street from her. I thought, *Oh Lord, she's going to talk my ear off now.* After a few days of organizing my place, I picked up Verna. I didn't tell her that I'd moved. I just asked her to take a ride with me. After we got back to my place, Verna asked, "Whose house is this?"

"A friend of mine." I knocked on the door like someone was inside then I opened the door and said, "Damn, no one is home."

"Do they always leave their door unlocked?"

"No, from now on it will be locked. Welcome to my place." Verna was happy to hear me say, "Make yourself at home." The first thing she wanted to know was if I had cable. I gave her the remote. Once Verna turned on the television, she watched it so long that it was too late to take her home. So before going to bed, I told her I would see her in the morning. About 7:00 a.m. on Sunday morning, Verna was still asleep and the television was still on. As I was turning it off, Verna said, "I'm watching that."

"Yeah right the TV was watching you. There is food in the fridge. Help yourself. I'll be back in a few hours. I'm going to church."

After church, I took Verna home. She thanked me for the day out, and I said, "Anytime. My door is always open."

After I got back home, I did some things around the house for Ms. Pamela. It was starting to get dark, and I needed to go in the house and get clothes ready for work in the morning. Tomorrow would be Monday, I hate Mondays. As soon as I got to work, everybody started calling my name. I thought, *Damn, it's seven in the morning. Can I get some coffee and clock in first? Thank you.*

After I finished cleaning the grounds, I got ready to do some work orders. Ms. Blue said, "D, can I talk to you for a minute?"

Ms. Blue was sixty-eight years old but acted like she was twenty-eight years old. I thought that I had seen it all until I saw Ms. Blue wearing skinny jeans and a booty pad. I was trying my best not to laugh.

"What's up, Ms. Blue? You go girl, with your skinny jeans on."

"D, can I borrow twenty dollars? I'll give it back when I get my check next month."

"Damn today is only the fourth, you just got a check three days ago and you want me to wait a whole month for twenty dollars?" She was begging me for a loan so I just gave it to her. After Ms. Blue went to her apartment upstairs Mr. Kelly, the security guard, looked at me and I looked at him; we both started laughing.

"Stella doesn't have anything on Ms. Blue," I said.

Then Mr. Peterson came flying through the lobby (that walking cane of his hitting the floor like a hammer hitting a nail).

The security guard said, "Slow your ass down before I give you a ticket," and we started laughing. One thing about the first week of the month is these senior citizens start moving fast. Just last week it took Mr. Peterson ten minutes to walk from his door to the lobby, but on check day, try ten seconds. One thing I've learned working around senior citizens is that nothing but their age defines them as a senior. Otherwise, they are just regular folks. For the rest of the day canes and walkers were on the move. This was the day after the first of the month.

That is the day of the month that I go to the bank for Ms. Lori, pick up Ms. Martha Madison and take Ms. Jane to the grocery store. They always ask me if I want something, I tell them to just get me some fruit, and that is how they pay me. While I was mopping the halls, my boss Ms. Kathy called me to the office. She told me that Ms. Davenport could not open her front door. I was trying to remember whom Ms. Davenport was, but my mind went blank.

After getting the spare keys and going to the seventh floor, I knocked on her door, at the same time called her name, and instructed her to stand away from the door because I might have to push it open. She said okay. I pushed the door open and discovered that the paint was making the door stick.

"You must be Darryl," Ms. Davenport said.

"Yes that's me."

"Are you married?"

"No not yet," I said, and she just smiled and in my head I was saying, *okay!* I told her that the door was fixed and I would see her later. She didn't say a word, she just kept right on smiling at me. After I got back downstairs, I asked Kelly what he knew about Ms. Davenport and he said she didn't come out much only on check day like most of them do.

"That's all you know?"

"What happened, D?"

"Nothing, I was just curious."

After I got off work I made my rounds for a few of the seniors I did favors for then I went home. The next day at work, it was about 8:30 a.m. and I was mopping the hall. Ms. Davenport was getting off the elevator. I told her to watch her step. She didn't give a damn about a wet floor because she walked right up to me with that smile on her face.

"Good morning, Ms. Davenport."

"Can I talk to you for a minute?"

"Sure."

"I like you, D."

"That's cool. I like you, too, like I like everyone else."

"You know I haven't had a man in twenty-five years. When I first saw you, a chill went through my body."

I thought, *Oh shit*, and then I cut her off from talking. "I would like to finish talking to you, but I have to mop the floor."

As I walked away, she said, "What's wrong? Is it because I have arthritis in my knees?"

"No."

"What is it then?"

I didn't answer. I just walked away.

After I finished mopping the hall, I walked to the security desk to holler at Kelly. "Man, do you know that Ms. Davenport hit on me?"

"D, don't let these senior women fool you. There are a lot of them here that would love to have a young man just like those senior men like young women. Shit you don't see them talking to the women in this building. They go out and find what they want on check day. So you better watch your back. You are going to have a lot of them hitting on you."

Every day for the rest of the month, Ms. Davenport was coming downstairs. Kelly and my boss started teasing me. They would say, "Your girlfriend was looking for you." I just ignored them. I would punch out for lunch and go to the craft room to play dominoes with the old timers. As usual they were talking shit, raising their canes at each other like they were about to fight, and drinking. But I enjoyed being around them. I could see myself at their age, so when I played dominoes with them I acted just like they did.

As time moved on Irene and I had become close friends. She was one of the In Home Supportive Service workers. She took care of Ms. Thelma Williams. I would go and see Irene almost every morning just to say hello.

Ms. Thelma said, "Why don't y'all get a room?"

I said, "We don't need a room. All we do is hug each other and say good morning, plus she's married and I'm not trying to break up a happy home."

Irene said, "Happy not even, a home is all that it is. He sleeps in one room and I sleep in the other one."

"It doesn't matter, you are still married." I gave Irene another hug and I gave Ms. Thelma one, too.

I went back downstairs to finish working. By this time, I had gotten to know all of the seniors that lived in the building. Ms. Blue would come at me like I was her man saying I need $10.00 while holding her hand out. I would ask her when did we get married and please remind me when I agreed to have you as my girlfriend. She would still try to get the money, she'd say, "Come on, D. I really need $10.00 and I'll give it back to you on the first of next month. You know I will."

"Your ass is almost seventy years old and you still run around here like a chicken. I'm not giving you $10.00. Peace out."

"Okay how about $5.00?"

"Ms. Blue, you are just like a cat. You feed them once and keep coming back."

Before getting off work, I got a call from a pay phone. I normally don't answer calls if I don't know whose calling, but something told me to answer this one. It was Verna. She was crying and talking fast.

"Slow down. I can't understand what you are saying. Now start over and talk slow." She said her daughter and her daughter's boyfriend put her out on the streets. I asked her where she was and she said at the grocery store up the street from her daughter's house. I told her to stay there until I got off work. A few hours later, I went to pick up Verna from the grocery store on Western Avenue and 110th Street. As I pulled into the parking lot, I saw Verna standing by the pay phone. I pulled up and told her to get in. As I pulled off, she apologized for putting me in this, but she didn't have anyone else to call.

"Don't worry about it, we are like family and no friend or family of mine will be in the streets if I can help it. Where are you clothes?"

"They put my shit in the garage. That's what started the argument. They told me that I had to keep my things in the damn garage. I said, 'So you're telling me that I have to get up every morning and walk around the back to get my clothes?' My daughter, Ms. Betty the bitch and my grandchildren started laughing like the shit was funny. Then that no good two timing alcoholic bastard Robert said, 'Yeah, walk your ass to the garage every morning' then we started arguing and he told me to get the fuck out of his house.

"I looked at my daughter and asked her how she could do something like this to her own mother. I reminded her that I had put up with her and those bad ass kids of hers for over two years, 'Two fucking years I put up with your shit. You all tore up my damn house every damn weekend plus your ass hit the streets and stayed gone six to seven days while I was stuck watching your kids. You tell me that you have nothing to say while this man is putting me out on the streets? You and he will rot in hell for this' then I walked out of the door."

"Well we have to get your things, so when I get off work tomorrow we'll swing by there and pick up your clothes."

"If they haven't thrown them in the trash by then."

"I hope not."

After getting back to my place, I told Verna that she could have the bed. I have a blow up mattress in the garage. After getting everything organized, I took a shower and went to bed. I was stressed out and tired. I woke up about 1:00 a.m. from the sound of the television. Verna was still up watching it so I told myself, "I guess I have to get used to this." At 6:00 a.m. I was up getting ready for work and the televison was off. I was shocked. Verna was out like a light so I didn't disturb her. I would just call her later and tell her to be ready when I got off.

I picked up Verna after I got off work. Thank God it was Friday! She got the rest of her things with no problem and we drove back to the house. One month later, I found a program that helped senior citizens. They told me to bring Verna in for an interview. The following day I called my job and told them I would be in late. The place was just a few blocks from my job, which was a good thing. After we got there, they told us that it would be an all-day process and they would take Verna home when they were done. So I took off and went to work. I was only fifteen minutes late.

All day I had my mind on Verna, hoping they could help her get back on her feet. An hour before I got off work Verna called me saying she was back at my place and would have to go back in three days. I told her okay and that I would talk to her when I got home. When I got to the house, Verna was asleep. I said, "Long day," and Verna's eyes popped open.

"Wow, I've never filled out so many papers in my life. Section 8, Social Security, low-income housing and I'm still not finished." What Verna was saying was good news to my ears. I knew that all of this was going to take time and that we would have to be patient.

Winter and spring had come and gone. It was now summer. July 4, 2012, the time for fireworks and the day Mom was born. I try to keep to myself on this day because memories get the best of me. As time moved on Verna was still going back and forth to the center and to the doctor building up her case. During this time, my job had become a part of my life. I was helping more people than I could count.

There was a man named Mr. Robbins in the building where I worked. I noticed that all the shoes he owned were old and had holes in the soles. I asked Mr. Robbins what size shoes he wore. I also asked him if he would like a new pair of shoes. A big smile came upon his face when he heard that question. "Yeah," he replied, "but it will take me a few months to re-pay you." I told him not to worry about it, just look at it as an early Christmas present. The following day Mr. Robbins was wearing his new shoes.

I know that eighty-five of the seniors in this building don't have much money left after paying their rent and buying groceries. So I do what I can to help them and I hope when I reach that stage in my life someone will do the same for me. We had a new tenant move into the building—Mr. English. He came to me for everything. I didn't mind helping him and he was so quick to reach in his pocket to pay me. I would tell Mr. English, "You don't have to pay me for these little things and whatever you do don't let anyone con you out of your money around here."

There are some good people here and some bad ones trust me you will meet them both. I knew from that time on I would have to keep my eyes on Mr. English he was just too quick to reach into his pocket. After a few weeks, I would see Mr. English every morning about 7:30 a.m. sitting in the craft room waiting for access services to pick him up and take him to the center where he would stay until 3:00 p.m.

This particular morning something was wrong. I could feel it when I looked at him so I asked Mr. English if everything was okay.

"Mr. Alonzo won't pay me back the money I loaned him," he said.

I shook my head. "Mr. English, what did I tell you?" He was holding his head down like a little kid. "I don't care if it was a dollar or a hundred dollars, don't let him get away without paying you your money. When you get back from the center, take care of your business."

Come to find out that Mr. English had loaned Mr. Alonzo two hundred dollars. Mr. Alonzo was an old con artist. He would have a pocket full of money and still ask people for a loan until the following month. Later that day I saw Mr. Alonzo in the craft room playing dominoes. I didn't say a word I just gave him that look. He asked me what's wrong. I still didn't say a word. I just walked right pass him. At 3:30 p.m. Mr. English was back from the center. I was standing by the security desk talking to Kelly. Mr. Alonzo was sitting in the breezeway with five other seniors just talking away.

After Kelly buzzed Mr. English through the security door, he was walking fast. He walked right up to Mr. Alonzo and told him he wanted his money back and he wanted it today. Through the glass doors, Kelly and I saw Mr. Alonzo's eyes get bigger than owl's eyes. Kelly asked me what was going on between the two of them and I told Kelly what happened. Kelly said, "Somebody is going to hurt Mr. Alonzo one day. He does that shit with somebody every month." It made my day to see Mr. English stand up to Mr. Alonzo. The next morning when I saw

Mr. English, he had a smile on his face. I just gave him a high five and mopped the floors.

Two months had come and gone. It was a Monday morning around 7:30 a.m. I didn't see Mr. English and his 8:00 Access Ride was out front blowing for him as usual. I knocked on his door and got no answer, so I went back up front to let the access driver know he wasn't home. Tuesday morning 7:30 a.m. once again Mr. English was not in the craft room when his access ride arrived, blowing for him. I asked Kelly if he'd seen Mr. English leave that morning and he said no. Something was wrong, I could feel it. I told my boss that I had not seen Mr. English for two days and that was not like him. She asked me if I'd knocked on his door and I told her yes, on Monday and today, but I got no answer.

So Kelly and I went to check things out. He had not told the office that he was going away for a few days, but no one had seen him for two whole days. After opening the door to his apartment, a very bad odor almost knocked me off my feet. I covered my nose with my shirt then I yelled out his name three times. As I looked around the room, I saw food and clothes on the floor. The top mattress was also on the floor. Still, no Mr. English. As I turned around to go out of the door, I checked the bathroom, but he wasn't in there either. I told Kelly he wasn't in there.

"What's that smell?" Kelly asked.

"There is food all over the floor," I replied.

As I was getting ready to walk out of the door, something told me to look on the other side of the bed.

"What are you doing?" Kelly asked.

"I'm going to look on the other side of the bed," I said, and there was Mr. English on the floor.

After Mr. English passed, I was waiting to hear about his funeral arrangements. After about a week had gone by I asked my boss Ms. Kathy if she had heard anything about Mr. English's funeral arrangements, she told me no. I asked her if he had any family that she knew of and she said that no one had come to the office and his emergency contact number on his application was no longer in service.

I said, "Damn," then she said if no one comes to get his belongings in the next sixty days they were going to send them to Goodwill. That was very disappointing for me to hear. Mr. English was a friend of mine and nobody knew if he'd be buried or not. After two months went by some company came to pick up Mr. English's belongings. There was no name on the side of the truck. I had no idea where they'd come from and there was never any news about his funeral. I just prayed that he was in a safe place.

As time moved on, Ms. Blue turned into Ms. Deebo. People started hiding their cigarette, lighters and money when they saw her coming. She came downstairs to the lobby asking for cigarettes and money and when nobody would give her what she wanted she would ask Mr. Kelly, "Where is Brother D?" He would give me up every time by letting her know that I was in the tool room. After dealing with Ms. Deebo I would walk to the security desk and he would be laughing, and I would say, "That shit is not funny. Pay back is a motherfucker."

After making my rounds it was lunch time and while I was sitting in the breezeway getting some fresh air an ambulance pulled up. I asked Kelly where they were going and he said he didn't know yet. I walked to the elevator to see what floor they were going to; it was the second floor. I was trying to think who had been sick that week, but no one came to mind. So I walked back out to the breezeway and waited to see who they were bringing down. About fifteen minutes later I said, "Oh my, God!" It was Ms. Deebo. We were all in shock. "Not Deebo," I said to myself. She looked at me as they took her through the breezeway then she said, "Bye, Brother D." The way she said it was like I would never see her again.

The first few days Ms. Deebo was gone everybody felt free but after a week had gone by I started to miss seeing her around. No one had any information as to how Ms. Deebo was doing. I was praying that she would pull through whatever she was going through and hoped that it would be a wake-up call for her to change her habits. After two weeks went by Ms. Deebo came walking through the front door she had put on some weight. I was happy to see her back home when she walked up to me I had to give her a big hug. I said you don't know how much I prayed for you. After Ms. Blue AKA Deebo went up to her room, Kelly asked me why I cared so much about people and that she doesn't care about her own damn self.

I looked Kelly straight in the eyes and said, "You're not the first person and you won't be the last to ask me that question. Nobody sees or feels what the other person sees or feels. That's what makes us different from one another. I have come a long way in my life. I've sunk to the bottom of the barrel so many times and come back up until I finally got it right. In that time I have grown to love myself, have faith in God and to see a person for who they are as a human being not for the type of person they might portray because of bad decisions.

"We are all made in the image of God and no one is better than anyone else. No matter the circumstances. Just because a person may be a drug addict or prostitute or even homeless or have AIDS you and no one else is better than they are. I also told Kelly about my past, how streets used to be my father at one time but my heart was still open. That is what pulled me out of the darkness. Everywhere I went people tried to tell me that I didn't belong there and it took over twenty years before my eyes were opened.

"I realized that I belong here as much as anyone else I also realized that I had to live my life in a better way if I wanted to be a happy person. Those twenty years of walking down dark roads was like being in the service, you have to go through training. There are over a million a day who get drafted but only a few who are chosen. I graduated from walking in the darkness in 1997 and that was when I was sent on my first task to the streets of Los Angeles, California."

As of now I am still working with senior citizens. Still taking clothes down to Skid Row and I will always enjoy helping others when they are in need. Where I go from here only God knows but I am ready to go wherever He sends me. I am no different from anyone else. Whether you love me or hate me, I will always be me. No one has the right to judge any other that is a job only for the Lord. God has His hands on me and I do my best every day to draw my strength and understanding from him. He has allowed me to complete this task. My story has been told. This is my life up to now.

Darryl Barnes, 2014

A Journey with the Homeless Pictorial

D. Barnes is standing next to the Space Shuttle Endeavour on the corner of 77th Street and Crenshaw Blvd. in Los Angeles, CA .D. Barnes is watching the shuttle during its historic journey to its final destination to the California Science Center in Exposition Park, Los Angeles, CA. The shuttle will become a major tourist attraction.